The Secrets of Romance

Ingredients of Love, Chemistry alert!

Doreen Kattah

ISBN: 978-1-8381513-1-7

Published By

LOVE ME WELL
Tel: +447941353132
Email: maamekattah@yahoo.co.uk

Printed in the United Kingdom.

DEDICATION

I dedicate this book to The Almighty God, the Son and the Holy Spirit, through the inspiration, wisdom, dedication and understanding given to me to write on this subject. All I am and have is not by my strength but by the mighty hand of God. Deep in thought and meditation you have endowed me by your grace.
LORD I AM GRATEFUL.

This is also in memory of you, Daddy, the Late Brigadier General David Crockett Kwadjo Kattah, for teaching me to never give up, but to persevere in all things with honesty and dedication always.

Contents

ACKNOWLEDGEMENTS

Writing THE SECRETS OF ROMANCE has been an interesting journey. The time, deep thought and research put into writing a book was harder than I initially thought, but it has all been worth the effort and more rewarding with the number of people who helped ease that pain, and the enduring relationships I have developed in the process. I can smile now at the completed work and say thank you to you all. Without your invaluable contribution, inspiration, moral support, encouragement and financial support etc., we wouldn't have come this far.

Thank you to the Gracious God who guided, directed and inspired me. I humbly thank You Lord for Your knowledge released upon me.

To my mother Cecilia Bouto and family, I say thank you for your support and understanding,

To Reverend Felix Ofosu Boahene who has contributed to my life through his kind direction and support,

To the entire congregation of Liberty Life Ministry for being a supportive family to me,

To Pastor Joseph for your support and prayers,

To Reverend Joycelyn Darkwah for your support,

Mrs Beatrice Asamoah Kwakye for your immense contribution to this book,

Mr Owusu Frimpong, Joy Yiadom, Isabella Malou, Winnifred Amoako, Margeret Aseidu and Mama Comfort Okai for all your efforts, encouragement and dedication to me.

To all my spiritual children,

To all who read this book.

THANK YOU.

FOREWORD

The Secrets of Romance is sure to make a vital contribution to the discourse on family and relationships that has been going on for some time now. Reverend Doreen's insight into this vital subject for could not have come sooner. As a man I feel this captures equally what matters to all aspects of relationships and men especially have often been unable to articulate and express their deepest felt emotions to their wives, partners and daughters appropriately enough because many of us simply do not know how. With this insight from this brilliantly written book, we now know how, and hence can go on to profess our love towards those dear to us much better. This will certainly go a long way to plug the gaping hole in most marriage and family interactions and will hopefully bring much needed healing and stability. I was surely blessed reading this book and I hope you will be too.

PASTOR MARK NYARKO
Mount Zion Revival Ministries, London UK
Host of Moments of Truth, Faith Channel Radio

Key Points

If something is factual, it is real and can be proven as beneficial or the better preference. Lives which are often based on the utterance of false and destructive statements and ideologies have resulted in dissatisfaction, to their quality of life, to the extent that even some have lost their lives as a result of wrong statements. A wife became depressed and committed suicide because her husband told her he had regretted marrying her and that she was good for nothing. These words disturbed the woman until she took her own life, leaving a note that read, "I don't think anyone cares about me, even my own husband. It is better I leave this planet. I am sorry I have to go." Such a sad departure.

Also a statement like, "what you do not know will not kill you" is detrimental to a person who believes in the literal meaning. I say drinking unlabelled poison or chemicals that are deadly will not unharm you because you did not know it, you will be harmed or lose your life as a result. Let us check statements before we put them into action.

My intention for writing this book is not to argue with any particular viewpoint but to provide provable facts and tested opinions upon which can be a credible foundation and a basis for practical decisions. These facts may have been practised or observed in our day-to-day activities or living. To live life based on principle or what is called authentic living, factual questions must be asked, and right answers received. Such information could be obtained by discovering a new perspective on matters or from having a fresh view of issues that challenge our belief systems. Statements which were once said to be true with time and careful observation have been rectified/revised to be untrue or not being the full truth. Some statements have been made to fit in a particular context or situation and is not fit for all occurrence or occasions.

Some old beliefs are very ethical but yet can point us to live a life of complacency. Complacency in an individual's life will make one lose their will to improve and self-motivation for greater personal achievement. On the other hand, you get used to things being done in the same manner irrespective of the hazards you are causing to yourself or people around you. Awareness is something that must be part of everyone's psychological compass, a kind of personal navigation kit. Careful observation must be done in focusing on your beliefs and approaches in other to reduce future problems. Some choices have been made and applied to our lives based on the available information which may not necessarily be true or right leading to problems. What problem can we solve with wrong information? In the world that we live in, wrong information has never yielded good results. On the contrary, the opposite has always been true.

These are statements that some people have lived their lives by, but I see the factual points to be:

- As it has been said: what you don't know will not kill you – I say what you don't know can kill you.

- Ignorance is a killer disease that can only be cured with accurate knowledge.

As it has been stated: True love never fails – I say True love can fade and fail if you don't work on it.

- As it has been said – Don't judge a book by it cover – I say the cover of a book is as important as its contents.

In the same way the appearance of a person is as important as their attitude or character.

- A folktale states – The future is unknown to no one – I say the choices you make today can determine your future. (Your future can be influenced by the choices you make today.)

- As it has been acknowledged – Silence is Golden – I say silence cannot always be golden. There comes a time when silence becomes a betrayal and one needs to speak up.

- The end of a new broom sweeps clean but old brooms know the corners. I say – society does not care for what you know but what you do with what you know. I prefer the new broom doing the work than the old broom just knowing.

❧ As it has always been said, experience is the best teacher – I say some teachers need to gain new experience, as some experiences are outmoded – which means advancement is better than just experience.

These factual points are to make you more aware of the other side of things. (God, the author of all wisdom said to His Disciples "let us go to the other side", Mark 4:22) try to move to the other side to have a clear view of things. As said by Debasish Mridha, "fear stagnation not adventure."

I say this with the wisdom of God – when you don't look to every side of the coin you lose sight of what is on the other side or what is in your hands. Think about this statement!

Don't live in a double-minded world but be abreast with time. Put on your lens, open up your mind and let's begin to explore THE SECRETS OF ROMANCE.

INTRODUCTION

TIME TO KNOW, TIME TO SHARE, take time out, the secret is out. Secrets are places where we hide truth; everyone has a secret; some secrets have been stored or shared. No matter how intelligent we may be, we don't have all the answers or know it all because secrets are a deep fountain of truth. Many yearn to share it. Tell me your secret and I will tell you how useful it is to me because not all secrets are beneficial to us. The secret romance is for your benefit. Sometimes what we claim to be the truth is not authentic, if the whole truth is coated and it coded another lie, not all attention must be given to that truth. My view of truth is that it is exceptional, and I want the truth! Nothing, but truth, that's what the secret to romance holds and is what I hope to share. Our freedom to the serenity of life is by what we believe and not perfection. Perfection is what we seek to have but is far from what we do. Just because we may have to stop wishing for or stop singing in its continuous regime and start doing something about what we desire. Facing your inadequacy and working on it is when you are heading towards perfection. We may lose our minds by pursuing it, but I believe truth in romance can be attained. Let us seek the truth in matters rather than perfection. The road to every successful life is based on revelations received and understood.

Sex has been a bait to lure many to unemotional ties where desire of the majority has been in limbo. Sex is a great city where many want to live to fulfil their sexual fantasies and desires without unanswerable questions such as,

- How can I reach my peek in sex or lovemaking?
- Will my high libido be accepted?
- Who can move me to the apex of my climax in sex?
- Does it matter if I don't have an orgasm?
- How can I be turned on?
- What if I don't feel like it and he/she does?
- Is it ok for me to fake it?

With these questions and unfulfilled desires, companies have manufactured sex aids to solve the problems associated with unfulfilled sex such as getting aroused. With the problem still unresolved, many have lost their sexual desire and sexual edge. Others have also admitted to faking orgasms.

Are you hungry for answers? Are you searching for what can satisfy your quest and hunger for the ultimate sexual fulfilment? If you are ready, this book THE SECRETS OF ROMANCE will be your guide to discovering and accepting who you are and your sexuality. Bringing passion back in relationships, freeing some locked-up desires and also helping others to update their sexual fantasies is what this book is about. It all begins with Romance.

Romance is the trace map to your heart's matriculation. When romance is out of the equation, then sexual fulfilment is denied. Light up romance in you, and you are on the road to great climax and undeniable satisfaction in sex. Romance has not been respected to it maximum, it has been downgraded, misused to some extent and is unheard of or unknown. This abuse of nature and romance has cut short enjoyment to sex. Some relationships thirst for romance and the thirst has not been quenched because of wrong motives and moves. If sexual fulfilment is just about sexual performance then all prostitutes must be awarded with gold medals, but the opposite is true. There is something more rewarding than sexual performance, this is called emotional intimacy, which can be derived from romantic fantasies and its satisfaction.

HOW CAN ROMANCE HOLD SUCH IMPORTANCE?

Theresa was a lady who had waited for many years to be noticed by a man who would be bold enough to propose to her. This was a dream come true, her prayers had been answered. This was the day she had been waiting for! She exclaimed, " At last my time has come. I am getting married!" Her previous demeanor began to change from being gloomy to that of a cheerful deer, for as the deer panted for water so her soul pants to be in the arms of her beloved.

The melody in her heart was, "I am in love." She sang every day as she saw her dream come true.

Finally, the day arrived, and with much anticipation she could only wish for brightness of everything. "My joy has been awakened; my branches are now bearing fruit of fulfilled desires." She called for friends, families and loved ones to join her to celebrate with her on her special day. On that day her love story was about to begin, as she walked towards the altar with much hope, aspiration and desire for the long-awaited future. She was so excited to be called "Mrs", that at least she would not be lonely anymore.

The marriage ceremony went well, everything was done to her satisfaction, family cheered, friends were happy. Everyone was so excited, for her day had gone well above and beyond expectation. Of course, the best was yet to come as the night approached. The night we all call **HONEYMOON**, with many facts I think that night should be called the discovery night instead. Many things do happen on such nights. Such as Theresa's experience, she was well prepared, she took out her lingerie singing, "let my love undress me on my bed", she was ready for everything that love would offer her, she was hoping to receive tattoos of kisses all over her body, drown in his romantic touches and fulfil her desires with his lovely sounds and words. Had I known, she thought to herself she could have waited for a better day than now. The pain and bitter pills she took that night remained with her for many years. She became a log in the bed for many decades.

As she took her catwalk down to the living room in anticipation of releasing what she had stored up for years in grand style, for Theresa had prepared for sexual intimacy by reading love novels and other intimate books. In her see-through nightgown with her seductive perfume all turned into fury. As she sat on her husband's lap, her hands stroking his hair, her panting heart was yearning for a touch and soothing words but instead she fainted when she heard him scream, "YOU PROSTITUTE! Where did you learn this from?" Her jaw dropped in amazement, tears rolled down her cheeks, as her husband walked away. What a shock, bitter discovery on a night which was supposed to be all HONEY turned out all disappointing. Theresa's heart bled from pain, disappointment, despair and discomfort, all that same night. Her emotions were shattered along with her self-confidence, her heart closed tight with a padlock to all advances to future lovemaking. Nothing could move her anymore; she had to switch the light off and close her eyes before allowing him (her husband) to pounce on her like a lion will prey on an innocent monkey for food for a few minutes and roll back after he gained satisfaction and gratification for himself. This is likened to an act of murder. Her heart had been murdered. The heart of a beautiful deer had been brutalized. She endured this crucifixion of abuse, and I will say, this was cruelty in the highest form. Will Theresa be able to hold her marriage vows until death do them part or rather be separated due to the lack of desire and the beauty of love and romance? Her lifetime expectations of marriage in reality ended in brutality, must it always be this way? How can romance hold such importance? Unaddressed issues on romance can bring divorce such as in Theresa's experience. It's true that divorce rates have risen beyond human understanding, so then, marriages would have been secure if only we had paid particular attention to our sex life and other areas such as romance, amongst others. It depends on how you look at it. Don't get me wrong there are multiple factors contributing to the breakdown of marriages, these are not grounds for arguments, there are many dry places, dry emotions, dry beds, contributing to the shortage of emotional fulfilment. "Christians make the best lovers" was a slogan used not long ago because there was a belief that Christians were more groomed for marriage due the counselling and pre-marital preparation that they undergo but can the same slogan be repeated today? Search yourself. For the times that we wonder to ourselves how can you make love with the same person for the rest of your life and still love it and be satisfied? Something must turn me on always. What is that? THE SECRETS OF ROMANCE.

CHAPTER ONE

What is Romance?

Back in the day when romance was seen as a form of temptation or a promiscuous lifestyle, when one expressed their passion, desires and physical needs to sex, Romance was forbidden. Sexual degradation was the ideal, some still hold that parochial mind-set that intercourse was for reproduction only and that you weren't meant to derive any pleasure from it. Why on earth some people are so scared of sex when the command has been issued, "Go have sex"? God initiated sex for married couples and for their enjoyment.

Is lack of romance that strong to break a woman or man's heart into total despair which in turn leads to the unspeakable spectre of divorce? What makes romance so strong that the lack of it turns aspirations into palpitations? The beautiful song that never got sung, dreams that were never fulfilled, desires that were never satisfied, places that were never explored in the end due to unaddressed shortage of romance, ended the show.

WHAT WENT WRONG?

This awful experience of my friend brought me to a whole different world, an eye-opening world, full of questions in my mind that I needed answers to before I began my journey of love.

Journey with me to find out what went wrong. Romance was zipped in the bag. It is time to let romance out of the bag.

WHAT DOES ROMANCE IMPLY?

Romance seems like a comedy in a fiction book. With many people having their own opinions about what romance should look like, feel like or be, they have made love suffer a brutal fatal accident of misjudgement and misunderstanding. Join the crew in finding out the mystery of what Romance entailed in THE SECRETS IN ROMANCE.

My opinion may not matter in this context as we want to find the true meaning of romance and its origin, backed by what we accept as the norm.

Romance is a genuine feeling from the heart that discovers passion. Passion lost, is genuine feelings uncontrolled. Passion is what brings the desire of the heart to know ways to sustain joy. Nothing is as important as Passion. No matter what you want to do in life without passion your mission is nearly impossible. Whatever you desire to have or do, be passionate.

A person can succeed at almost anything with the power of passion. Passion put into romance becomes a remedy of successful desire. Passion should be expressed genuinely and should not be faked. When you lose passion, you have lost it all. Passion can be transferred by sharing. Sharing and showing what you have is a means of making your passion known. You can never stay in love without passion. Likewise, you can't eliminate romance from the love scene and still call it love, it is nearly impossible.

Mr. Isaac had a very beautiful wife called Rebekah. The King of the city of Philistine asked him about her. Mr. Isaac said "she is my sister" because he was afraid to tell them she was his wife. He thought they might kill him so they could have her. He lied. One day as King Abimelech, the king of the Philistine looked out his window, he saw Mr. Isaac holding his wife tenderly (romancing, caressing, smooching, petting, etc.) the King immediately called for Mr. Isaac at the sight of the passionate affection shared between Mr. Isaac and Sister Rebekah. He then said, this woman is your wife. Why did you say she was your sister? Mr. Isaac having no words to back his action, had to admit the romantic love they shared was as real as a panting dog on heat. He couldn't deny, romance cannot be denied if it bubbled from the soul.

This romance bears witness to the affair between two people. How can two people in love not feel the chemical attraction between them? Romance is substantial in every erotic relationship. Indeed, partners often wonder why their relationships fail, where those loving feelings have gone, or why they don't feel what they used to feel anymore. Some partners are disconnected from each other, yet they live together. The emotional attraction of the relationship must be rekindled. Romance is a crucial element to happiness in relationships. In as much as some long for romance in their relationships, they do not have a clue as to what romance is or how it's implemented. Our decreased effort in spicing up the relationship will always lead to breakdown and stagnation of emotional support and/or physical disconnection. Romance must be tailored according to our needs. Know what works for your partner and also for you. I say this again, what works for your partner and you. Always seek the interest of the recipient. Most of the time we fail in the demands and delivery of romance when we are adamant about what makes our partner happy or what sparks their heart. Simply know and apply what makes your partner live on "cloud 9". Creating romance in a relationship becomes easy when you become mindful of the desires of your partner. Customize your romance – put in your own twists and make it your handiwork. Keep your romance alive by working it out to suit you and your partner. In some cases, in an attempt to work on our relationship, we adopt from others, things that are not relevant to our needs, therefore the knowledge acquired becomes irrelevant. Copying good things from people may not necessarily be good for you if it does not generate a positive response. Also, we often rely on x-rated movies to gain "experience", and we end up not getting the same reaction or satisfaction as seen in the videos and other materials. These people are actors and actresses, performing. A working romance is one that is always anticipated, desired and appreciated. Be imaginative to enhance our happiness and enjoyment in our relationships. I ask, can you create a menu for food? If yes, then you can create a great recipe of romance for your recipient and you. Making all ingredients relevant in your menu for romance will make your lover or partner attached and more connected to you. Many such results can only be achieved by discovery; discovering your spouse or partner's needs should be your number one aim in bringing satisfaction. When you lose sight of discovery, you lose the element of sustaining the joy in your relationship. Marmalade, for example, has many ingredients but without the citrus effect marmalade is not marmalade; likewise romance in a relationship. The ability to sustain romance lies in the secret of discovery, which is the one thing that moves your spouse into action, the action to respond to your demands of love or affection. Affection can be gained and lost, provided you know what button to press and how to maintain the operating button. Chances have been given and also taken but none yielded the right fruit because preparation was not adequate. Don't live by chance and hearsay but live with the aim of knowing your spouse and their every desire and remember no two people are the same. Many couples have outgrown each other and there is no more connection or a spark just because they have failed to learn. Connection to the heart is the basic connection and the most important of all connections you need and it must be worked on to bring fulfilment in other areas of your life.

Romance can help you have:

- The bond you need,
- The fun you desire,

- The gestures you need,
- The hilarity you need,
- The adventure that will inspire you,
- The freshness you need to stay in love.

The continuity of every lasting relationship is a dual purpose, which connotes the involvement of the two parties. One-sided relationships always collapse easily thus the saying it takes two to tango. This may be used to mean that some things need the active cooperation of two parties, hence my paraphrase that the tango dance is never done by one person and therefore one needs a SUITABLE dance partner in the ballroom.

Denying each other's feelings will lead to the drying up of the juicy part of every love affair. Romance feeds the soul and brings nourishment to the body. It also awakens our strong feelings of enthusiasm.

GESTURES

Gestures can also spice up romance. Whilst many gestures can deny romance, others also invite romance. Sometimes one may not be aware, but they give wrong invitations by the gestures they make, thus causing a lot of damage and misunderstanding in relationships. Don't you think the norm must be looked into before being applied or copied? A gesture is dangerous to use when we don't actually know its meaning. You must employ your gestures as pure acts of love to show your partner that they mean the world to you. Do unexpected acts of romance to show your partner you care. There is something sweet and sensual about surprising your partner with romantic gestures that warm the heart, irrespective of gender.

THE MEANING OF GESTURE

1. A movement of part of the body, especially a hand or head, to express an idea or meaning.

2. Gesture is a form of non-verbal communication or nonvocal communication in which visible bodily actions communicate particularly with movement.

3. A gesture is speaking with your actions. There are a lot of romantic gestures, you can express. A passionate kiss, a love note in a pocket or purse, romantic text messages, a bouquet of roses, a love song, travelling miles to go whisper a lovely word in the ears of your love, holding hands whiles walking in the streets.

Love notes such as:

Being in love with you makes me live life fresh every morning.

You are my lifeline.

I am smiling so much today just thinking about you.

You've made me taste the best love ever, you taught me the true meaning of love.

I will regret living if we are not living together. You are my source of joy.

We belong to each other. I wouldn't fit anywhere else.

I say show me your romantic gestures and I will tell you how deeply you are in love and connected.

Let us use our gestures well without giving wrong impressions. I remember years ago when a lady received an unexpected marriage proposal owing to the gestures she demonstrated towards a man. Gestures are very strong messages and if well understood will boost pleasure immensely, but if not may cause havoc and disruption. Gestures spice up the heart for further advancement. I long to be in your sweet embrace which is "anhelo estar en tu dulce abrazo" in Spanish.

ROMANCE

Romance may differ from one person to another depending on their preference and their level of attraction towards the other, but one thing must be attributed to all, which is the attraction of the heart.

All accreditation should be given to Romance since without it sex becomes boring and undesired making the relationship lose its spark. Romance is the fulfilment of the heart's desire being explored in different forms to meet the desire of the body.

As the Oxford dictionary defines romance as "a feeling of excitement and mystery associated with Love."

- Romance is intuitively referred as one's expression of deep desire of love to connect with another person intimately.

- Romance is a mystical affection controlled by emotions.

- Romance is the trace of the heart to affection and attachments.

- Romance refers to the action and feelings of people who are in love, portraying behaviours which are very caring or affectionate.

- Romance is raw passion and tenderness of the heart to kindle love.

- Romance is Precious routines of the heart to connect.

- Romance is the booster of the needs of the heart.

- Romance can be termed as a decorated expression of love.

- Romance is the icing that entices you to eat the cake.

- Romance is the honeycomb that stores up passion in the heart.

- Romance is the cry of the heart for affection.

- Romance is the dew that wets your love canal.

- Romance is the fire that warms the cold heart.

- Romance can be a great weapon or bait to fight the unwilling heart to submit.

- Romance clothed in persistency is the hammer that breaks the stony heart.

- The regiment of romance can collapse whole twisted emotions.

THE ORIGIN OF ROMANCE

With all this said and done, what is the origin and history of romance? The word romance originally stems from the Latin word "romant", which means Roman manner. It is also a type of story that was written in the Roman language.

Romance in essence can be traced back to the seventeenth century when it was to describe imagination and inventiveness in storytelling and also characterized scenery and paintings. The written stories were normally about love and adventure. The word romance was associated with beautiful occurrences linking to love or matters of the heart.

Romance became a word normally used in description of love affairs and occurrences pertaining to love. It was also, a way of life with reference to the love stories of the Romans. Romantic culture generally expresses and exalts mankind's energetic, creative and expansive tendencies to love and predicted occurrences of love. It's also a word used to represent connecting two hearts in their innermost desires. Intelligence and reasoning are indeed valuable but cannot achieve on their own what passion in the mind and heart can. Romance makes passion have a home to live where feelings are concerned. Romantic attraction helps every relationship to aim towards sexual fulfilment. Humans long for attachment and emotional bonds to each other because as humans those bonds help us to survive. We instinctively develop loyalty and affection for those who show the most loyalty and affection towards us. Though passion, romance and sex often make us do ridiculous things, sometimes regrettable, we cannot deny the powerful feelings of love in the moments of sharing or receiving.

In the ancient world romantic love was seen as trivial. History makes us aware that romantic love was looked upon as sickening, where love was not the normal basis or foundation of marriage. People in the olden days did not marry because of their feelings for one another, and feelings didn't matter in the ancient world. Marriage was meant for baby-making and sound finances. Marriage was arranged by families not because the partners liked each other. It was also not because they loved each other but at the time marriage was designed to economically promote the survival and prosperity of both extended families.

WHY?

There was no time for romance, and certainly no tolerance for any time-wasting on being with each other kissing and caressing. There was also no room for potentially risky behaviour that was associated with because romance was seen as leading to complications.

Time was only allocated for the farm business; there were fields to plough and cows to feed. Everything you did had to be done for the simple sake of the survival of the family, not personal aggrandizement.

The need for romance was only accepted if the other party was able to provide financial support.

There was little or no knowledge of romance, because they didn't know any other way of life. The self-willed business of family survival was causing more harm than good, bad choices were made in terms of love, but good choices were made workwise. Feelings of the heart over time couldn't be suppressed anymore; living with someone who had little concern for your emotional needs, made people prone to anger. Few years down the line married partners realised their partners had different ambitions or life goals that were contradictory to their own. They held different opinions and beliefs about life compared to theirs. Their happiness was being drained, for you not to be loved for who you were but rather what you had was truly pathetic. People in conditional, toxic relationships and marriages used to struggle to express love to each other or didn't love each other. The love was either one-sided or there was nothing there at all. They spent all their life and time pretending. Some were simply afraid to be vulnerable or alone, since love could put you in that state or would require your selflessness. People were seeking ways to liberate their hearts from belonging to the wrong people and also free from being a family merchandise. Many fought the hostility of the heart, traded for pain, decided to go through temporary pain to free themselves from future agony by rebelling from the constitution that caused their grief.

A Romeo and Juliet story. A major influence of ancient tragic love stories, most notably of the Roman story of Pyramus and Thisbe; who despite their families hating each other and preventing the lovers from being together just through a crack in a wall were able to whisper their love for each other. The end was bizarre. But in all true love indeed won.

True love is stronger than anything else in the world. And this is the kind of love we are all hoping to find someday, with a happy ending, of course.

A few centuries ago, romantic love was not that famous due to the ignorance surrounding it but growing awareness has had an effect on the danger of not knowing each other intimately, thus creating greater opportunities for couples to hurt each other. The great liberation of romantic love has brought incredible love experiences into the world. It's also brought the necessity for an honest approach to relationships that accommodates less pain of spending the rest of your life with someone your heart doesn't desire to be with and creates room for a healthy, respectful and enjoyable relationship.

I say everybody needs Eros in their relationship for its survival. Relationships have complications on their own but a lack of romance in marriages and relationships can greatly complicate matters in the love scene.

CHAPTER TWO

You as an Individual

According to Dr. Juanita Bynum, you need to be *you* – and to do this, you must know your identity – who you are as a person – as an individual – even if this means embarking on a search to locate the person whom you once were – or maybe always sought and still aim to be. This idea of you as an individual – a separate and unique entity – a person like no other person before, alongside or after you – someone totally distinct from all those around you (even though you are, of course, part of the community/ society and linked to everyone else in myriad ways) – and needing to break free from what others want you to be or do – to find yourself – this idea or concept is sometimes referred to as 'individualism'. Of course, Dr. Bynum was not concerned about theories and what anyone may want to call the things she says. But it is important to at least understand the things that I am about to tell you in terms of theories, so that you will have a better grasp of the role your individuality plays in unlocking for you, THE SECRETS OF ROMANCE. As she wisely points out, we are all intricate – yes, each one of us – so, having an understanding of how complex people can be – can contribute to the way we see them right now and will fill us with a new respect for them. Where better to start having an understanding of those complexities than with yourself as an individual, so you can understand the people we relate with.

One of the many criticisms against the Christian way of doing things and understanding the world is the great emphasis on individualism. Individualists (that is, those who support or propagate individualism) have been said to incorrectly and even irreverently, portray institutions such as the State and even the Church as evil. Another is that individualism puts too much faith in the power or ability of individuals to think clearly, make rational or 'correct' decisions and do good. A further criticism of individualism is that individualists believe that free will should be unfettered. Critics believe that if each person is allowed to use their God-given free will without any restrictions this will lead to great atrocities. It has also been noted that individualism places probably too much emphasis on the importance of personal freedom – the freedom to do what we like with our bodies, for instance – or the freedom to explore our sexuality and sexual desires with other (consenting) individuals. Individualism is also said to erroneously encourage flat-out competition. Economically, this is viewed as dangerous not only to capitalism but to workers' interests, especially as it would appear to perpetuate the Darwinian doctrine regarding survival of the fittest. In the context of this book, it can also be perceived as putting certain people – particularly those who may not have the means to compete effectively, at a distinct disadvantage, since as the old English adage states: 'to the winner go the spoils'. Individualism has also been shown to place individuals above society which therefore means that no matter what cultures, religions and laws require, the individual – not the community – or even the Government/State, has the final say in how they run their own life. As you may agree, some of these criticisms are quite merited. However, as with everything else human, there are no perfections; therefore, we must not allow the fear of what individualism does wrong or is allegedly doing wrong, to hamper the need to explore – and grow in our individuality. With the help of the five (out of many more) bright minds below, let me take you through what it means to be an individual in love or romance and why you as an individual your desires matter – as well as realising who you are as an individual and how it can help you and your partner (who don't forget, is also an individual) enjoy true love, sweet romance and of course, great sex. As an individual where do you find sex?

SEX IS EVERYWHERE

Sigmund Freud (1856 to 1939) was one of the earliest people in modern times, to study how the human mind works; he was also one of the first people to link the behaviour of individuals to sexual thoughts. He also 'discovered' that every person – even babies, have erotic thoughts and have more recently (though less intellectually) argued, it is unnatural to restrict sexual expressions and interactions. Note that people can be sexually stimulated using any part of their bodies – depending on the individual so that sexual enjoyment need not be restricted to the use of genitalia but can also be vocalised, demonstrated and imagined. There is also the tendency for people to end up romantically, and/or sexually, with people who remind them of their dads or mums – especially if they had such a good relationship with their parents that they miss it so much. There are individuals who are locked in a continuous battle against their sexual urges, who seek answers and freedom. Today, his ideas are not as influential as they used to be, having been largely contradicted by Maslow and even more by Rogers below. It is in fact impossible to seriously discuss human behaviour, especially in romantic or sexual matters, without involving him. Sigmund Freud highlighted the individuality of each person, explaining that we all have from time to time, thoughts that would shock any person who knows what is on our minds. He said that while most of us would condemn sexually abhorrent behaviour such as paedophilia, bestiality and homosexuality, many of us harbour deep within us, thoughts quite similar to the actions we are disagreeing with and/or attacking (Freud and Strachey, 1905). He postulated that while our actions reflect what is on our minds, they say even more about things hidden far below the surface and rooted deep in our past, sometimes in childhood or even babyhood. If you want to understand the secrets of romance and to explore your individuality this is the place to start. In understanding ourselves as individuals, it is important to know what makes us different and why we do what we do. Now is the moment to ask questions about our lives and personalities. This is especially the case with romance and sex. You are an individual of worth but you have a lot of exploring to do. Don't be afraid of exploring your individuality and fantasies!

It is true that we all have minds, but the mind is so unreadable and therefore the best way of understanding and even influencing people is by observing and controlling their behaviour.

Skinner's operant conditioning theory holds that people's way of behaving is affected by what we hope to gain or enjoy and what we fear we may lose or suffer – in other words, rewards and punishment. In effect, Skinner's argument was that if people see that something will make them happy or avoid pain, inconvenience or discomfort, they are likely to behave in a way that enhances or at least entrenches this pleasantness. In a like manner, we are always moved to shy away from things that we see as dangerous or unpleasant.

Skinner proved this through the use of several experiments and concluded that the greatest influence on our behaviour is neither our minds and what is in them, nor our past and sexual hunger as Freud argued, but something more visible, tangible, malleable and its consequences (Skinner, 1938). If we take Skinner's ideas further, we would see that there is something for you to learn about you as an individual. Of course, Skinner, like every person before him and those who have come after, was not perfect, yet there can be no doubt that he had some points which sound interesting in his theory. People trying to change difficult or challenging behaviour such as in schools and prisons, still use his theories to this day. More relevant to THE SECRETS OF ROMANCE is the fact that

Skinner has given us reason to look again at what works and what does not in our romantic and sexual relationships. He has also led us to ask; *why* and *why* not? These are important questions in any relationship, especially when things do not seem to be going right – but even when they seem to be at the best. You see, if BF Skinner is to be believed, whatever your partner does to or for you, the things he or she tells you, brings you, shows you, gives you or asks you, are influenced by your own reactions whether real or imagined, actual or perceived. There are flaws to Skinner's argument of course – for instance, can't people love just for love's sake? Must our relationships really be about what we expect or do not expect? But we are not looking at the drawbacks of Skinner here: we are more concerned with the way he can help us unlock the secrets of romance. Two of the oldest sayings about relationships are very reflective of Skinner's theory as they suggest that our elders noticed – long before even Skinner was born, that operant conditioning is real (even if they never called it that). It is said that *Diamonds are a girl's best friend and that the way to a man's heart is through his belly.* Would you agree with those statements? What do you think influences your romance and desires as an individual?

RESPECT AND APPRECIATION DO WONDERS

Carl Rogers (1902-1987), propounded the person-centred theory which says everyone wants to be happy, fulfilled or 'actualised' (Rogers, 1967). Rogers is particularly significant in THE SECRETS OF ROMANCE since he focused partly on romantic relationships (Rogers and Gloria, 1965). Rogers postulated, that in relationships, every person wants to receive from the other person three main things referred to as 'core conditions' for the relationship to be established and to flourish: genuineness (i.e. sincerity or 'congruence'), empathy and to be respected – viewed as having worth or value – what Rogers called, *Unconditional Positive Regard* – UPR (Rogers, 1967). The person-centred perspective also holds that each person, no matter who they are, has dreams and visions of who, where and what they want to be (Wood, 2008). Rogers agreed that how we see ourselves is not always how others see us (for example, I might think I am friendly whereas people see me as boring; or my culture might say that I cannot join a particular profession, while I feel that such a role in life is what I am specifically suited for.) but what matters to us is not how others see us, but how we see ourselves. Given that according to the person-centred perspective, every individual has ideas of where their happiness lies, Rogers further argued that who better can tell you about what is on someone's mind than that person? Therefore, every person is the expert in their own life. If for example, you fall ill, doctors, pharmacists and nurses, etc., can tell you what they think is wrong with you and maybe what they see as the solution to your perceived problem; however, it is your choice, your right and even your duty, to make the final decision on whether to accept what they say or not. This can apply to everything else: so in terms of romance, your culture, society, family, etc., may say it is wrong to kiss or fondle, but if you think for yourself, you will realise that such choices are not theirs to make, but yours since both of you are intelligent enough to know what you want and what is best for you. Of course, there are drawbacks to this way of seeing things – the key questions include but do not stop at: *If we have so much free will where do we stop? How can we even tell when and where to stop? And who can truly say with conviction, that we all know what we want, or that we are the real experts in our own lives, or that we don't need someone to direct us and tell us what to do?* So, I do not believe – and therefore will not advise you to accept, that the person-centred approach has all the answers in life or even in romance. The important thing, nevertheless, is that as Bynum and even Chapman imply, we recognise ourselves as individuals and never be afraid to go for what we want – our fulfilment, our happiness, our dreams

YOUR NEEDS HAVE A VOICE

Abraham Maslow (1908-1970) like Rogers after him believed that each individual wants to be happy in life. He studied human behaviour and came up with the view that ideas such as Freud's and Pavlov's were probably full of merit, but they were ultimately flawed. He therefore conceived the concept of what he saw as a 'hierarchy of needs' (Maslow, 1943). Maslow stated that every person is an individual and as individuals, there are things we need which if we do not receive, will leave us rooted at a certain level until we achieve them. He suggested also that these needs are universal to all people. Effectively, our needs affect our ambitions and dreams, thus with the fulfilment of each need starting from the most basic, we can look up and see higher things which we would now feel free(r) to explore. For example, I may want to become very successful in my career, and may want to spend most of my time on my career improving myself but as a person in a relationship I must make time for my partner, or be there to support my family when the need arises. Such as in times of sickness. Therefore, I would focus more on finding a cure, than on which university to attend. In a romantic sense, this would also mean, that a person who wants to enjoy a good romantic or sexual life would need to address certain basics. for instance, if I am battling starvation or acute insomnia, it would be difficult to concentrate on giving my partner the best he or she would want from me sexually or romantically.

So, while sex and romance might be important, peace of mind will always come first. As you may have guessed from this explanation, Maslow believed that our needs (and dreams) are stratified. Where one must come to the level of knowing themselves and striving to be better with who we are and what we have. Building your self-esteem is a very essential aspect of our lives that we must all develop. Your self-esteem should rely upon your personal qualities and character, and not on your physical qualities alone. You should take strength and confidence from your actions and achievements instead of your appearance.

Remind yourself of your best of attributes and skills and be proud of what makes you unique. Though we are all far from perfect, be yourself and don't be afraid to show the best side of you. Embrace your individuality, don't compare yourself to anyone, because you are different. There is no one like you, You are the only You that exists. Focus on improving on your weaknesses and also keep polishing your best side to make you feel valued, loved and fulfilled. This goes a long way to affect your sexual ties. Your awareness of yourself always pushes you forward and makes you stand firm when others are losing it. Laugh at some of your mistakes and also know that gloomy days will come, and when they do, develop the very attitude that will defy the bad moments by doing what will refresh you or what you love most, such as singing, watching TV, sleeping, etc. Your strength is never in your weaknesses but your strength is what beautifies you. Get locked up in your strength and equip yourself in that. Keep in mind that you have a lot to offer.

LOVE LANGUAGE

Do you know that as a person, you are multi-sided? Yes – there are several sides to you. Psychologists refer to people in terms of *poles* – thus the term 'bipolar', while theologians tell us about *parts* wherein we speak of the body, soul and spirit. The truth is that we are all deeper and more complex than any person can explain. When it comes to romance, there are as far as I know four sides of you. In this section we're going to look at one of those: your love language. Discovering and remaining aware of your preferred love language is an essential secret of romance. But before we go further, ask yourself: *What does she mean when she says: 'Love language'?*

'Love language' simply refers to the way we express ourselves when we want to demonstrate affection or act romantically. People have different ways of speaking their love languages and this in adults is particularly unique in each gender. Have you ever found yourself in a position – say, during or after an argument with your dear one, or while to get a difficult point across, that things would be better – in fact great, if only your dear one could just understand what was on your mind? At such times, you know deep down inside you, that if only your darling could get a better understanding of how you were feeling, she or he would stop being so difficult – fighting you for little or no reason – yes, they would come round to your way of thinking and you both could get back on the smooth road of having and enjoying a sweet, sweet – really sweet romance. So, you get the picture.

The work of love languages is to let us understand how our significant others think in terms of affection. Love languages are compasses that help us navigate the complex (and sometimes even murky) world of love. You've got to know and accept that as we are each different, we all have our unique understanding of love. What love means to one person may actually be expressed differently by someone else. When two people come together in love, since they are two different people, there will surely be differences in expression between them – especially the expression of feelings. Being aware of the way we express love and affection – then building an understanding of how our darlings also express love and affection can have a very strong influence over your relationship. You may not believe what I am about to say in the next sentence, but it is as true as and as real as the words you are looking at right now. Being aware of love languages – both yours and your dear one's is probably one of the simplest and quickest ways of growing your relationship.

The term 'love languages' has origins in traceless antiquity, having been used in different ways and by different people through the years. The term was popularised, however, by the erudite American pastor and relationship counsellor, Gary Chapman through his books, several of which start with the words 'love language'. However, this book goes beyond Chapman to remind you that human beings are all similar and yet quite different. It is not about insisting that you are fixed in one position. Instead, I want you to understand that each of us has been blessed with the ability to speak several love languages. I do not think any person is incapable of speaking all the love languages, but I am convinced that most of us have the love language(s) we prefer – the one with which we feel most comfortable. So, what is yours? Which one do you find easiest or most at home to use? Let's look at some of these. If you have ever read Chapman's books, you may notice some similarities here – but you will also see some marked differences. It wouldn't be any use just recycling and presenting everything he said here if I did not have anything new or different to say.

To start with, Chapman writes that there are five love languages. It is my position that since seven is the number of completeness and love is the one word that captures the Essence of God more than any other word (in fact, we are told that: "God is Love"), there are not five love languages, but seven. I also believe that to love truly, you must be able to understand and maybe even speak all seven – yes, even though you may prefer to focus on or use one, most of the time. I've arranged them for easy recollection. I understand the seven love languages to be:

- Submission
- Beautiful words
- Caring gifts
- Dutiful or sacrificial acts
- Expressive touch
- Focus and
- Glowing or special moments.

Now, let's see what each one of these entails.

SUBMISSION – The old Biblical saying that "Obedience is better than sacrifice" when combined with the Scriptural Admonition that we must "Submit to one another", tells you something marvellous about love languages. There is an old West African saying, that "for two people to enjoy their relationship, they must each learn how to 'act foolish' for the sake of peace when the other 'acts wise' – because when everyone demonstrates how smart they are, nobody will live with the other". Thus, it is important to have an understanding of this love language. In my experience, more relationships break up due to people lacking humility and submissiveness than anything else. You will be surprised to know how many people are still in love even after breaking up with their partners (Relate GB, 2018). They are in love – but will never go back, because of the constant state of war that took place in the relationship – a state that was as much due to the lack of submission as anything else. Love is not a competition and it is not a game for keeping scores. This means therefore, that when people learn the language of submission, they acquire other attitudes that go with it: they are humble, peaceable, diplomatic, positive, friendly, optimistic, good listeners, considerate and willing to make concessions. "Love" as we are told, "does not insist on having its own way". Being acquiescent doesn't mean accepting everything though: it's more about wisdom.

BEAUTIFUL WORDS include what some see as 'words of affirmation' wherein we remind our darlings that we hold them in such high regard and they are the centre of our world. (Gary Chapman) But if you have ever been in love or romantically engaged, you will agree with me, that words of affirmation are never nearly enough: we want to hear more – we want to hear something deeper, sweeter and more sublime. "Sing them over again to me – wonderful words of life" (Reese/Wholesome Words, 2018). Some of us love to hear such things – we need to be flattered. Affectionate words might sometimes involve stretching things a bit or finding sweeter ways of saying the obvious. Whatever be the case, affectionate words are a very important and powerful love language. Writing poems or songs, singing and including your loved one's name in the song, writing nice things to them, etc., all fall into this category of 'beautiful words'. Beautiful words have the capacity more than anything else, to create what so spectacularly captured as 'Fantasy' – a world away from the world – a place where only both of you dwell – and thrive. Although we are not all poets and orators, you will agree with me that everyone can say something nice about someone else – and most of us don't mind hearing lovely things about ourselves over and over again! When such loveliness comes from the heart and the one we love, oh how truly delicious it must be!

CARING GIFTS are another language altogether. I am yet to see a relationship that began without the giving (at some point by at least one partner) of gifts. The thing about gifts is that they can say quite a lot. At first, gifts would say things like: "I am interested in you", "I like you a lot", "Please notice me" and so on. However, as the relationship develops and you begin to know your lover better, you should begin to get better at gift-giving, choosing gifts that make more meaning and are a lot more eloquent – gifts that continually emphasize five truly powerful words: I *care – I really do.* But receiving gifts is just as much a part of this love language as is giving. Imagine how it feels for a gift to be rejected! I have known people to fall out or drift apart over gifts not appreciated. You may even have come across someone who is sad because "no matter what I get for her/him, she/he is never satisfied". Gifting is more than symbolic: it is intrinsic. The simple truth is that human love and affection cannot survive without the application of this love language. Of course, there are some of us who may say that we are 'not gift people' or that we are not good at choosing the right gifts, but as one author points out, it is better to give – *give something,* than not give at all. The act of gift-giving should always be done with the aim of leaving a lasting positive impact and to create lasting precious memories for you and your partner. What does all this tell us? It tells us that gifts are an essential aspect of love and a very powerful love language indeed. I will go as far as to say, that even if you cannot speak the other languages, this is one you will need to learn. Of course, like I have said all along – and as Chapman continually points out – just as do many others before and after him, you may have other love languages with which you are more comfortable. However, whether you feel comfortable with this one or not, you will need to speak it from time to time, remembering that as the Bible states, gifts not only open doors, but bring us into contact with greatness. Likewise gifts connect us to people we like or want to get know better. A person who cannot speak or understand the love language of caring gifts is virtually not connected. Remember though, that if you only want to receive gifts, you are being unfair and selfish, while if you are in the habit of wanting to give always but never receive – often dissuading or discouraging your loved one from giving to you, you are displaying ungodly behaviour. Caring gift-giving takes thought, time and talent – but it is more about showing that we care. Caring gifts say to our significant others that we consider them so precious; therefore, we don't consider anything too much for them.

DUTIFUL OR SACRIFICIAL ACTS are another love language which can be quite potent. Just as in the 'normal' languages we speak, you find them related to others so that understanding one may help you understand the other (e.g. the Bantu, Akan or Latin tongues where although forming hundreds of languages, if you understand one, you will most likely have no difficulty understanding at least a smattering of the rest within the group), this love language is closely related to the preceding one and therefore understanding how to speak one will help you develop your proficiency in understanding and speaking the other. True love requires sacrifice – the act (in the context of romance at least) of foregoing things in order to please or benefit the person we share ourselves with. You see that this is also about giving, even if it's not about the actual giving of presents to your loved one. People who speak this language do not worry too much about the inconvenience. As Shakespeare so succinctly puts it: "the labour we delight in physics pain" (Shakespeare, 1599).

EXPRESSIVE TOUCHING involves physical contact where lovers fellate, kiss, fondle, copulate, etc. Expressive touch is for many of us the ultimate love language – the one which seems to say it all. It is so important that many people will hold back from speaking it until they know they will get something very precious or valuable in return (e.g. marriage, an engagement ring, certain assurances, etc.). How often or rarely this language is spoken, often indicates if things are going north – or south in the relationship. This love language is probably the quickest, most visible and most tangible way of telling your partner how you feel not just about them but about the relationship. Chaucer's character the Wife of Bath declares that: "I will use my instrument as freely as my Maker hath it Sent" – an example of how this love language works – and even an instance of combining love languages – beautiful words and expressive touch.

FOCUS is the love language where we give our significant other all our attention or as much of it as we possibly/reasonably can. In their timeless duet and ballad, Lionel Richie and Diana Ross project this love language powerfully as they croon: "You mean the world to me". The essence of this love language is to demonstrate to the 'hearer' or 'listener', that you feel you cannot do without them. This is not the same as being desperate or obsessed, neither of which is healthy; it is more about making the person the centre of your world and showing them that you expect the same of them. It is also about listening to what they have to say, understanding them better and ensuring that we are not left in a position whereas Carson's group puts it, we discover that "little things I should have said and done, I just never took the time" – even though "you were always on my mind" (Carson, et al, 1972) or as the band 'Mud' would add: "I wouldn't listen, to things you had to say" (Chapman and Chinn, 1974). People are speaking all the time, and this is especially the case in romantic relationships. Focus enables us to decode better what the other person is saying and to get our own message across to them in the language they best understand. Focus can be argued as actually the key to maintaining the fire of passion in our relationships.

GLOWING OR SPECIAL MOMENTS is what "happens when you're with me" as the indomitable Dolly Parton puts it or as Albert Hammond states, "the creation of a special world in which you and your dear one – even if for a fleeting moment, feel the world doesn't matter – it's just all about the both of you. Note that everywhere women and men are confused about what is healthy, mature, interdependent love". Much of this confusion and its maelstrom of breakups could be dissipated with the sharing of special moments. Often this can be found on holiday or vacation, but we can't possibly have holidays all the time – even if we could afford both the time and the cash. As a love language, glowing moments call for greater investment than the intermittence of going away to somewhere nice (which may not turn out to be that nice after all). "Okay – so, what is it all about then?" you might ask. What this love language is about is rising to the challenge of using your God-given creativity. A special meal, times of prayer, a night out and so on, can all fit into the category covered by this very special love language. Glowing moments can be both stimulating and arousing, but they also give you time and space to reflect, to refresh and even to refrain. Glowing moments are called that for a reason: they make time glow around you and nothing else matters.

When you know what your partner does and don't care about, it's a pretty big eye-opener. For example, for years, I've been giving my significant other small gifts to show that I care. I put a lot of thought into those gifts, and I loved surprising him. It would annoy me when he'd receive them and just say, "Oh cool, thanks," and then set it aside. That was not the reaction I wanted. By giving him a gift, I was saying, "I care about you," and "oh cool, thanks," is not a good reply to that.

When I realised "gifting" wasn't his love language at all, everything suddenly made a lot of sense, and I learned to show that I cared in ways that spoke to him. And as a result, when I do give gifts, he now understands that that's my way of saying I love you, and it means more to him now. What matters most to you?

As Chapman points out, there are different "dialects" for each language, too. For example, my primary language is quality time, but I also express and feel affection through Words of Affirmation and Physical Touch to some degree.

On the flip side, it's useful to know how you don't express affection. I ranked low on Acts of Service, and it helps to understand this as a blind spot. Let's say a friend does me a favour and they give me a ride to the airport. This isn't a big deal to me, so I might brush it off too quickly because it is not my love language. Similarly, I might be terrible at doing favours for friends, because favours don't matter much to me, so I assume they don't matter to anyone else, either

In short, knowing what makes you tick and what doesn't can help you empathize with people a little better.

Of course, the concept is also helpful in simply expressing your love in the best possible way. For my fiance's birthdays, for example, I'd always put a huge amount of thought into his physical gift. Now that I know quality time is more important to him, I cater to that instead. I put more energy into planning birthday trips together to the cinema or lovely recreational resort rather than whatever physical gift I'm going to buy him.

You can use love languages for other relationships, too.

I've found that the concept of love languages helps pretty much any relationship, not just romantic ones. It's useful to understand what matters to people.

For example, I used to get angry at my brother for being terrible at keeping in touch. He rarely called, and it hurt my feelings. But then, we'd get together at family events and have long, meaningful conversations, and everything was great. He'd tell me how much I meant to him, and I'd feel reassured. But then he'd go back to being terrible at keeping in touch, and I'd get my feelings hurt all over again.

It took time to realise that his "love language" is 100% Words of Affirmation and 0% Quality Time or Acts of Service. (Gary Chapman) It seems strange to me, but that's him, and that's how he expresses (or doesn't express) affection. Once I got that, his lack of calling stopped hurting my feelings. And it works the other way, too. Recently, he complained that my Dad and I always want to talk to him on the phone and he doesn't understand why.

"I hate talking on the phone," he said. "So, I don't do it. I don't know why that hurts people's feelings."

I joked, "Because when you don't keep in touch, we think you don't love us anymore." "Oh dear," he laughed, and since then, he's been better at reaching out.

It's worth noting that your love language might vary depending on the person, too. My brother might speak a different language in a romantic relationship than he does with family. And while I need quality time with my partner and family, I don't necessarily need quality time with friends to feel like they care or vice versa.

It can help in business, too. Business Strategist Marie Forleo says the love languages concept is her "secret weapon" in maintaining a happy team. As a leader, she finds out how each person on her team feels appreciated, and she can then motivate them accordingly.

Chapman even wrote a follow-up book specifically aimed at the workplace: "The 5 Languages of Appreciation in the Workplace". They're pretty much the same, but his explainers are translated for professional relationships rather than romantic ones. However, you can probably translate pretty easily on your own by simply taking a look at their behaviour and how they respond to situations.

Overall, it all comes down to knowing what's important to people so you can understand, empathise, and work with them a little better. Everyone is different. We all have different life experiences; we come from different backgrounds. It makes sense that we communicate differently too.

Love languages can't fix everything, of course. They're not going to solve your joint money problems, for example. They're not going to make your in-laws more tolerable or get your partner to help out more around the house. But the concept does go a long way in communicating better, and we all know how much that matters in a relationship. Love language helps to understand the needs of your beloved one whilst you get involved in the matters of his/her heart. Helping to appreciate little gestures in a relationship helps to manufacture new ideas to make things happen.

Don't give gifts that you like as a person but make more effort to know the gifts that speaks to the heart of your beloved one. Gifts always make the heart go tender, use them wisely.

Expressing affection through spoken affection, praise or appreciation. Acts of Service: Actions rather than words are used to show and receive love. Receiving Gifts: Gifting is symbolic of love and affection. With this love language the speaker feels affection through physical touch.

YOUR RHYTHM

Another secret of romance is *rhythm.* Knowing or discovering your rhythm is a good place to start, but if you want to enjoy your romance – and hopefully great sex, you must never ever stop there. Instead, once you've known your rhythm, you must know how to apply it effectively, so that it becomes part of the wonderful God-Given equipment you have for ensuring that you and your significant other share a fantastic love life like no other. But let's not get ahead of ourselves here; as the early bird told the late one: first things first. So, to start with, what really do we mean by 'rhythm'?

The term rhythm is generally associated with poetry, music and dancing; in each case, it can be taken as referring to a defined or clearly detectable pattern of words, musical notes and/or sounds (Oxford Dictionary, 2015). Rhythm has also been referred to as "a regular movement or pattern of movements" (Cambridge Dictionary, 2013). When change occurs in a regular manner such as the clockwork-like change of shifts at military installations, we can also use the word 'rhythm' to describe it (Oxford Dictionary, 2015). As with everything else in life, there is no perfect definition here, but you get the idea. Taken together, I would like to describe *rhythm* – especially in the context of romance and sex, as the things we do which demonstrate a pattern and in so doing, produce a sweet almost musical effect to which both partners in the relationship (or activity within the relationship, such as love talk, sexual intercourse, romantic writing, etc.) can relate with ease and in step or in tune with each other. So, in other words, rhythm as a secret of romance is all about what vibes you produce to keep you attractive to your mate and in which she or he can feel safe and comfortable, happy and thrilled. So, now that we've had an understanding of what rhythm means – particularly in the context of romance, the next question would be: *What is your rhythm?*

You may not know it, but rhythm is a part of our daily lives. Rhythm is as present and as real as Monday, Tuesday, and Wednesday and all the other days of the week; it is as ubiquitous as the air we breathe, and it is as undeniable as the ground beneath our feet. In other words, rhythm is everywhere. In our day-to-day lingo, we often say things like: "your sense of rhythm" is this or that (e.g. wonderful, poor, interesting, etc.); we indicate or detect rhythm in the movement of athletes, the actions of animals, the vagaries of the weather, etc. In fact, every person has a sense of rhythm. Yes – you have it, I do too and so do all your neighbours, friends, colleagues and so on. The rhythm of each person has a great amount of influence over their desires. The really interesting thing about our rhythms is that within each person, there are numerous other rhythms that combine to produce the main one. Our bodies have their own rhythms, our voices have rhythms unique to them and even the way each of us speaks has got its rhythm. Rhythm is often the element that makes us move along with, or give ourselves over, to a particular song or form of music and person; rhythm is there even when we laugh, chat or pray; rhythm is also a reflection of the consistency with which we do things. Rhythm determines your speed level. Your rhythm is a regulator of how fast or slow you are. When it is fast, then it has to be really fast and when you choose to slow things down, then it has to be really slow. This is usually because when you are determining your speed, some of us want things to happen quite fast, while others would rather have it all slow. In a romantic sense – and even sexually, there are those of us whose rhythm is such that if you really want to slow things down with them, then you might discover that nothing happens for them: it's like you are wasting your time. Conversely, for those whose preference is to move slowly, the same applies in reverse. In other words, nothing happens for them if you go at a pace with which they are not comfortable.

The entire romantic process is determined by rhythm. Some people like to woo or be wooed slowly; others would rather skip the entire process if they could or definitely shorten it if that was the next best option, giving a turbocharged nature to the act of wooing or being wooed. This principle of rhythm is undeniably also – some may say *especially*, the case with sex. During sex, some people want it slow, while others prefer it faster. Rhythm is present in your love song – thus, when you compose it – whether it is written, sung or simply acted out, we all write love songs with our hearts – so when you compose it, rhythm is at the root of it. It is through rhythm that you are best able to stir up and communicate your desires. When a good love song is composed or listened to – when rhythm is at its best, it stimulates – it stirs up desires in both the composer and the listener of the love song. One composes their love song in the heart with the state of their rhythm, though the heart may be silent there is always something going on there, the best is when you are able to listen to the rhythm of the heart and flow with it, it stirs up their desires. Rhythm in romance is a great combination to steal the heart. When you introduce rhythm into romance it becomes the captivating force that willingly hands over a heart to you for control, it steals the heart for you. Your rhythm is what brings you to moments of insanity in romance. A little insanity will help to make some climactic noises or moans, screaming, heavy breathing, silence, to further it into dirty talk when you are turned on. Some noise turns almost everyone on, but others are a total turn off, just a piece of advice for you, you should never force yourself to make any noises in the bedroom if you are not the moaning and noise type, if not you will turn the whole experience into a dramatic scene and a total turn off. The woosh, the ooooh, the Aa! Aaa, hmmm! Etc. helps. Moans and screams can be part of enhanced positive sexual pleasures, some like the sexy voice exchange that whispers and purrs with heavy sighs of the intensity of excitement, moaning of pleasure. Knowing what you want and able to express that will ignite things in the bedroom. In reaching your climax there are physiological changes that occur in the body. Excitement mounts, palpitations of the heart increase, the skin becomes warm, and almost every part of the body becomes sensitive to touch. At this point the face grimaces as if in pain, you groan audibly and loudly, all in excitement.

The stimulant of sexual appetite or climax flows from your rhythm, when you cannot control anything anymore, loosening yourself for penetration in lovemaking, moving further to the point of orgasm, when you just allow things to flow. Rhythm is your enhancer and your easy prediction; when you are in your rhythm, love signals can be detected, you become easily predictable by the gaze in the eyes.

Rhythm is what makes you respond to your feelings. Your rhythm is your transparency. Your rhythm is what separates your desires from another person's desire. Your rhythm is what makes you relax or arouses you. Also, it brings back passion and frees locked up desires. People have desires that they are slow to manifest. Some people due to fear, can't express passion to others because they think it will not be accepted so they hide their sexual desires. There are things that hinder us from enjoying romance such as not being yourself and blocking away your desire for romance. THE SECRETS OF ROMANCE aims to remove the shutdowns and make romance more a part of our daily goals and lives. Your rhythm is your map, it works on your heart, rhythm is what makes you respond to what is happening around you. Your rhythm, the trace to your heart as a map leads us to a particular place where you desire to be. Romance and your rhythm are very important to life and a way to your satisfaction and enjoyment. If our partner could read your rhythmic plan well and trace the needs of your heart almost half of the problems in this world would be solved. Do you agree with me that our heart has needs that must be met? When the needs of the heart are not met, it carries worries, troubles, pain, anxiety, etc. into daily activities.

CHAPTERS OF A ROMANTIC HEART

YOUR REALM OF FANTASY

Your realm of fantasy is as important as your realm of reality. In the classic *King Solomon's Mines,* we see a group of men embarking on a joint mission but each with a separate agenda. The interesting thing is how despite having different motives, they manage to work together and head towards the same goal. What is probably more interesting though, is that each man's agenda is based upon fantasy, a dream or a wish. But yet they put their individual fantasies aside and emerged to fulfil a task Most interesting of all is the fact that the dreams all come true more or less, despite a whole range of difficulties, some for better, some for worse. As per Love Quotes "There is no journey upon this earth that a man can't make if he sets his heart to it. There is nothing ... that he cannot do ... no mountains he cannot climb ... no deserts he cannot cross ... if love leads him". As you can see from that very insightful quote, love is the guiding force that makes it possible for you to traverse your realm of fantasy. A person in love does not understand the power of barriers. Nothing can hold them back. Looking again at what we have learnt earlier, you will see that your individuality is very important in romance. In effect, you cannot begin to enjoy love in any of its forms be it sublime romance, established marriage, or earthly sex without glorying in your individuality. Interestingly though, your realm of fantasy may be created by you, nurtured by you as well, of course, treasured by you, but it never totally depends on only you. In romance and even during sex, whether you are a woman or a man, your realm of fantasy encompasses not just your ideas and imaginations, but those of the person you are with. This part is what Vatsyayana alludes to in asserting that: "(though) a man loves a girl ever so much, he never succeeds in winning her without a great deal of talking". Why should he have to do so much talking? The answer is simple but not. It is not just that women love to hear men talk because woman are stirred up by words naturally, they love to hear exciting words. (many women would tell you they prefer that or they shut up!); it is because when a man talks to a woman while trying to win her heart, he usually comes into his own as a builder of dreams and fantasies, creating new pictures in the mind of the woman or enhancing the ones that she has. Everyone wants to hear affirmations of their sweet side or things they could be better at. Proper communication is the cement as well as the pillars that hold the relationship together.

It is important though, not to let your realm of fantasy be the only realm you dwell in. This is because, "fantasy can lead us to choose romantic partners for the wrong reasons". If you ask my advice, I would say to you, that dreams and Fantasies are good, but we must have our feet on the ground and dwell more in reality in addition to fantasy. Your fantasy must link to reality and not a Cinderella movie. Why is this so? It is because no one is perfect, but some fantasies create or seek perfection. The problem then is that we begin to expect things of the other person based on our fantasies; where the person is unable to live up to our dreams, this could lead to disappointment and therefore having a negative impact on your relationship.

As I said, fantasies and dreams can be good. What would we be without them? Almost everything ever invented or achieved, began as a fantasy. Your realm of fantasy should therefore make it easier to spice up your love life. You must however remember not to shut the doors to your realm of fantasy so that your partner can enter and be part of the fantasy. This of course entails a lot of talking, including what sometimes is referred to as 'sweet nothings' and 'pillow talk' and also digging a little from the past to smoothen the present beauty you want to create. It also takes us back to the bit about your love language – because your realm of fantasy is linked to the love language you feel most comfortable with. We are reminded too, that love is meant to be fun – romance should be fun – sex should be fun. Engaging in sexual intercourse and romantic encounters are so much fun, and the fun must be maintained. Anything fun could however, invite unwanted guests and situations into our world of pleasure and therefore we must also exercise caution when engaging in it not to open doors to intruders. So being realistic mustn't include being staid or frigid. Above all, it does not permit having fantasies that cannot be shared. In the 'Pacesetter' classic *Too Cold for Comfort*, a Christian lady got married to a man who happened to be well, let's say, not as passionate about Jesus as she was. While they were dating, she was the epitome of fantasy: sweet, doting, lively and all. He in turn, matched her in every way as he was among other things – strong, thoughtful and reassuring. But right from their first night of marriage, things began to head south. This was mainly because of each person staying in their own realm of fantasy and not opening the door to let the other in. The man in the story had fantasised about sex with reckless abandon, while the woman had fantasised about sex after a long prayer kneeling by the bedside; the man had hoped for a regular dose of sex, the woman had dreamt of sex only when babies were to be made; the man had hoped for boundless physical intimacy including kisses and hugs to no end, the woman had imagined a life of cooking and serving – but no touching. It was a cold wet night, the sight of his wife getting ready for bed was sufficient stimulation for him, the mood was on for lovemaking but to the contrast, the wife was only ready for bed, every advances to hold, cuddle, kissing the wife leading to romance and sex fail because she just wanted to be left alone. After many attempts the man gave up very angry and unsatisfied.

You can imagine where this was heading. A few hours after the man's heart cooled down, he called the wife and addressed the problem, the story ends with each person allowing the other into their realms of fantasy and then both of them managing to share a common dream which involved compromise – a bit of prayer here and a bit more sex there. Some women fail to understand this male fantasy (more and more sex). This common misunderstanding probably has kept more loving partners from learning to reach simultaneous orgasms than anything else. Sex is instinctively the most universal drive in men during their early years of marriage, whereas for women it is a potential appetite that can be cultivated.

A lovely sexually responsive wife can be a great asset to her husband and vice versa.

Every fantasy is a dream that needs to be worked on, there is the need to learn and feed your fantasy to come true. Romantic fantasies are different for everyone. The feeling, the tone, and the theme of romantic fantasy influence your passion. When butterflies begin to fly in your stomach and a kiss turns you on it opens you up to reality and the desire of your every being asking for more. Fantasy is complete when you move from secrecy to revelation to sharing and fulfilment.

Everyone has a love tank that may be half-full, empty, complicated, or completely full, whatever state your tank is, it still needs to be worked on and maintained.

Fantasy is your picture of exciting romance. Romantic fantasies almost always go hand in hand with sexual arousal and lustful imaginations. Romantic fantasies awaken love.

Fantasy is something important in our love lives, it might be missing in us, romantically shut down, in a state of confusion or dead in us. I say there is a need to intuitively awaken our fantasies.

TYPES OF FANTASIES

1. **COMPLICATED FANTASIES** – creating the wrong expectations for real love and romance. Get to know your partner or the person you feel affection for and ensure they feel the same. On the other hand don't overthink it and don't rely on assumptions. The desires and feelings should be mutual.

2. **TRANSPARENT FANTASIES** – this is what evokes strong emotions, you can never have a proper romance without transparency – transparency is what opens or closes you up. Open up to your partner, let them know what you like, love or don't want and together build on your own fantasies.

3. **EMOTIONAL FANTASIES** – this is how I want to be treated when excited, upset, or feeling low in myself. Sometimes I want to be cuddled and sometimes I want to be left alone. Remember love and fantasy are always learning processes and not all days are the same, we have sunny days and moody days whatever day or mood it is, emotional fantasies must be fulfilled.

4. **SEXUAL FANTASY** – this is how you want to be connected to sexually. Before you make love, during and after sex, how do you want to feel? Vulnerable? Feeling like a baby, be pampered, left unattended or ignored? Everyone is different and may respond differently after sex (But being ignored after such a pleasurable moment is not the ideal way, for as much as you can show affection after intimacy cuddling, stroking and the like.)

Before lovemaking, most men want to feel and be treated like kings whilst women want to feel and be treated tenderly. Whiles some may want to be dominant and in charge or play a role, all in all, ensure that you and your partner's sexual fantasies are satisfied.

5. **MENTAL FANTASY** – This is how the brain is wired to receive love signals. Your brain should be stimulated to identify the non-verbal advances or communication of sexual fantasy made by your partner. You should know when your partner needs you without having to say so.

6. **PREPARED FANTASY** – the dreams of love you have prepared to suit you. Before anything happens how do you entice your partner to prepare him or her for what comes next and preparing for what you want to receive? Preparation is more important than having desire. This is a sign of invitation to mate.

7. **THE CLOCK FANTASY** – this fantasy is the unreasonable fantasy, also called the chameleon fantasy, changing your desire at the sight of every new thing such as learning something new from a movie, or picking a new lifestyle which may not necessarily be suitable for you which is also being unsure of what you like as a person. People with such fantasies are not easy to please and mostly do not know what they want.

Fantasy on the other hand can be healthy or unbalanced. Though we might paint a perfect picture of our fantasy world, it is mostly based on administration or the state of the heart. It is also not a shock if some fantasies lead us astray or lead us to choose romantic partners for the wrong reasons.

Wrong fantasy bonds can be very dangerous to a budding relationship. Attraction is the core foundation to romantic desires. Without attraction there is no arousal on the part of both sex parties. Attraction must be on an equal level for the couple because improper attention can gain improper attraction. Any attraction without boundaries creates wrong desires and imbalanced love which has no genuine sense or basis. For you to be genuinely attracted to some you must first be yourself or learn to know the true side of the person you are falling in love with. Attraction must start with honesty to open up effective communication.

Vice versa, proper attention to someone or something can lead to a very desirous romantic attraction.

Outward attraction cannot be equated to the attraction of the heart, though very necessary in the evolution of love. Attraction is said to have gained its grounds when the sight of a person brings the heart to beating louder than its normal speed and also make you come alive within yourself and joyful. With all this I say this out loud, "sexual attraction can be planned but the chemistry that comes with it cannot be planned. sexual attraction can sometimes be faked when some people do all the right things for the wrong reason like enchancing your physical beauty by dressing to impress, makeup, using arousing or seductive perfumes, and also talking in a particular way. This may help a person to be attracted to you or create signs that that person is attracted to you sexually."

Sexual attraction is more than just a physical boost; it travels from the physical to the attraction of the heart. Attraction may start from the physical, but it must find its foundation in the heart. Attraction is the connection of the heart.

Every attraction starts forming when you come in contact with an uncommon physical treat that takes a person to astonishment. A decision begins to form in the head for advanced formal or informal contact.

Attraction is the lead way to commitment because one must possess some attraction to lure companionship. Without attraction there is no connection. People can be connected to different things and characters. The appalling character of a person can be the baiting factor for someone's love. How ironic, the way the heart responds to love and nature. The attention of the heart to something demeaning can also turn to the uprising of proper recognition and falling in love with that heart you pay attention to, regardless of their shortcomings. It is said in the old days, "one man's poison is another man's meat". Don't underestimate what the heart can fall for. Most have lost contact with their physical point of attraction, just because the heart was misunderstood or was mishandled by another inconsiderate heart. The pain began and the passion was lost. Attraction opens the door for fantasy, fantasy on the other hand can generate more fun in relationships than expected. Once you know your realm of fantasy you begin to flow in areas where you become complete to open up for love. Ideas will flow from your mind to your heart and cause you to live the dream you desire to live without any excuses. Love is very beautiful when handled with care and due respect. Enjoying your love is what opens you up for future advancement. Don't deny yourself of this beauty but take time to understand the way you love and what leads you to love. Don't discard your realm of fantasy but hold it, learn it, and use it for your satisfaction. Satisfaction can only be gained when you know yourself and why you do the things you do. Smile at yourself and say, I am going to know you better. It is your sole responsibility to know yourself and pass the information on to others who desire to be with you. Living in harmony is when you accept who you are and allow others to travel into your world without fear. Personality traits are also important in your love world. What is your trait? Do you know it?

Don't be adamant about your own self, learn more about you, for you have more to discover about yourself. Use you to make yourself happy instead of using others. Play with yourself, talk to yourself. Smile at yourself, this will lead you to accept and see yourself in a new light.

Fantasize and don't let anything stop you. Fantasy is simply a pleasant situation or event that you think about and that which you want to happen, fantasy is using your imagination to build the world you want to live in. But living alone in your world is as boring as living in a desert with no one to talk to or no water to quench your thirst. Sharing your fantasy with the heart that is ready to accept you for who you are, is a moment you don't want to deny yourself. A shared fantasy is moving from the desert lifestyle to live in a palace full of riches. Fantasy begins in the brain but must not stay in the brain. Just as sex also begins from the brain and must be despatched to the body for performance by a healthy means. The mind should be prepared in the advances of sex, when the mind is ready it makes intimacy easy. Fantasy is a means of preparing your body to respond to sexual triggers that aim at sparking fulfilment. Fantasy can be mute when it is shared with unprepared hearts or minds. Many people have lived the ignorance of their fantasy and have prepared themselves to doom in the contest of sex and enjoyment.

A couples' survey made some years back revealed that most couples are unaware of their sexual fantasies. Be in the light and forget about the past, to march forward is knowing all about yourself to enable you to enjoy your life. As sweet as fantasy may sound, it has its loophole, where one may apply or live in the wrong fantasy and miss the sweet sensation of what fantasy can offer. Know the types of fantasy, and work on your desires when you fall in love. I want to debunk those myths, that fantasies are not necessary or unimportant in our love affairs. In fact, we can achieve more with fantasy than missing out. The imaginary world can influence our romance by digging into areas in our lives where we have denied our emotions. Emotions can bring much positive awareness to our memories being good or bad if we handle them well.

Trigger the romance in you, use it and love it. Most importantly love yourself.

SEX AND YOU: YOUR SEX DRIVE

Sex is a weapon, a car and a chief driver who drives its passenger to unknown destinations when proper precautions are taken. Desires have been dispatched to containers holding on to unfulfillment. The journey of life has been bitter and prolonged in a sweet by and by, a melody without rhythm.

There are couples who are sexually dysfunctional because of locked-up desire due to dissatisfaction or selfishness, that's not good enough.

Whiles some are smiling in the pool of love and lovemaking, some are deeply sinking to the bottomless pit of loneliness and dissatisfaction.

What song should I sing? Should I have known better or what should I be aware of when it comes to sex? A wholesome appetite for lovemaking should be created.

Sex, a three-letter word but BIG in nature and in understanding. We all are sexual beings; I believe that sex and sexuality should be a positive experience for everyone. Your sexuality, your social background, your beliefs, your educational background, your taste amongst many forms a very important part of you, which makes you who you are. Without an understanding of who you are, you cannot understand sex and its satisfaction. Why? Because it is you who makes, sex but not the other way round. Sex is only a word until you put it into action. Action in sex must cooperate with our nature to make it complete. Basic information about sex is to engage in sex which you are comfortable with (Your nature or your style)

Sex can be referenced to people, the two major forms of individuals, the species on the basis of their reproductive organs, male or female but am talking more than just their gender, hot sex as an action word, the art of sex, defined as sexual intercourse is principally the insertion and thrusting of the penis, usually when erect into the vagina for sexual pleasure. (Wikipedia)

Sex is uniquely designed by God for enjoyment and procreation formed by your own experiences, life lessons and emotional bonds. The importance of sex and its meaning are completely unique to every man and woman in their own feelings. Sex demands a lot more than just feelings, it takes your attention (mind), your spirit, and your entire body. This means it takes everything about you to engage in sex, that is why you are important when it comes to the sexual act. Your art of sex is your act of freedom, sex is an independent decision but always needs co-operation with your partner. While most of us are sure that we like or love to have sex, some of us also haven't spent much time thinking about what happens physically and spiritually. Once you take part in sex, it affects your whole being. There is a deep spiritual aspect to sex and physical pleasure that comes with it. Whenever two bodies engage in sex, there is an exchange, and a union takes place. The souls become united whether you know it, like it or not. I may not want to go more into this topic because it is not my subject matter but will be discussed in my next book, THE POWER OF SEX. This is just a hint to highlight my point. The best way to become a great lover is to know your own body first and be willing to invest the time and energy to know your partner's body, thereafter knowing your individual G spots. Good and mature sex is a road map to good mental and physical health. A well satisfied Sex awakens the divided soul living in confusion. When the heart seeks satisfaction, different solutions are made available. Sexual drive is one of the ways to bring satisfaction to the human heart but few realise its value., As stated earlier sex can be a weapon, car and the chief driver. The mobility of every car requires something called fuel to cause it to function, so sexual drive is the fuel that moves a car from one place to another or in the other sense it is the fuel that moves the desire of the heart to perform sexually. No car can move on its own without fuel or electricity. Motor fuel is used to provide power to motor vehicles. Such as sexual drive is the motivator that increases the desire for sex, there are different ways one can be motivated sexually. Becoming yourself is the most important factor to enjoy sex, walking in your unknown desires can kill your sexual passion and slow down your sex drive. Every car is powered by different fuel, some cars move by petrol, others diesel, ethanol fuel, electrical power, etc. May i ask, what type of fuel are you? Using the correct type of fuel for your vehicle is normally recommended by your car manufacturer for the best result, just as in humans, your sex drive can be powered by different factors if sought for. Mostly it is inborn, already in you. The "manufacturer" has already planted it in you. It is God given and needs to be recovered or discovered to enhance your sexual appetite or sexual desires. Controlling and using your power of sex for your satisfaction can only be achieved by discovering your sex drive. Don't shut out the discovery of your sex drive, dive into and live it for your pleasure. The assertion of your sex drive is your diadem, that differentiates you from the many gallopers. Proper use of your sex drive causes the mind to be more in tune to nature, whereas some drives may lead others to be promiscuous, living a life of shame. Having an uncontrollable sex drive is potentially dangerous to your way of life. One must learn to rule over their sexual desire and not to be controlled by emotions. Promiscuity is not a life to glory in; in fact it is more of a loose life. Losing in the game of life is not a place anyone would like to be. In other words live to influence yourself positively. This makes your drive to sex very important. A gas station gives gas to a car for the enhanced use of the car not for its depletion. The furtherance and proper use of your desires or drive all depends on how you use what has been given to you. Don't be ashamed about your sexuality but rather delve deep to learn more about your sex drive.

You cannot be moved by something if it does not please you. On the other hand, some are driving cars that are not theirs,in essence some people have allowed other things to repress their feelings so they do not own their sexual gratification. (meaning living in a territory that you don't have control of or people's opinions, religious suppression, and cultural deformity have kept you in stigmatized position... How Sad.. free yourself.)

Own your sex drive!

Gaining knowledge of what pleases you is the best university you can be trained in. Invest in advancing in developing knowledge of yourself.

As we saw earlier in this chapter, sex (and the drive for it – also called 'libido') is usually at the root of most romantic relationships almost from the start, libido is your motivating factor to sex. According to Wikipedia libido is defined, "as a person's overall sexual drive or desire for sexual activity".

Your libido sometimes lies dormant but powerful and present, even outside romance, influencing our daily lives – including somewhat surprisingly, the way we relate with people e.g. even our parents. Sex drive in humans is very powerful, presumably but not yet irrefutably proven to be stronger in teenagers and young adults and men presumably have a higher libido compared to women. This part of human desire has attracted and/or should attract constant but probably wholly unnatural and even unwholesome regulation by religion, culture, families, governments, ourselves, etc. Before I launch into this last segment, I would like us to consider one question: why do we have sex drives?

Why do we have a sex drive? There is a reason humans crave sex. It's part of our body's primal drive, in other words, our body craves it because it feels good. The fireworks you experience between the sheets can also light up our brain.

Studies show that more sex and better quality sex may contribute to happiness and there are more chemicals involved with sexuality than we know what brings excitement and connects us to have a special bond with our spouses.

There's one part of our desires which is the underlying factor. That which jump starts our emotions or causes as to do what we do. This mechanism is called hormones. Hormones in humans will be looked into to buttress my point. You cannot talk about desire without taking a look into the subject of hormones.

A regulatory substance produced in an organism and transported in tissue fluids such as blood or sap to stimulate specific cells or tissues into action in the body is called hormones. Hormones release chemical messages to the brain and its reproductive system by influencing the function of the immune system, growth such as sexual mood or development which also alters our behaviour. Hormones affect our body function, but our hormones don't make us crazy or irrational beings. Most disruptive behaviour is attributed to hormonal imbalance, instead of the improper use of the mind. I do not lose sight of the fact that our hormones have control over our mind but not to cause us to reason immaturely, characterized by our own nature or the way we do things.

Hormones are boosted by the nervous system to influence behaviour to ensure reproductive success. Hormones in our bodies are our jumpstart for moving our emotions to connect with adrenaline, the adrenal glands also play a large part in producing those hormones. Adrenaline is a natural stimulant made in the adrenal gland of the kidney. It also stimulates the heart to beat faster and work harder and promotes blood flow, adrenaline triggers the body's fight or flight response. The body's ability to feel pain also decreases as a result of adrenaline. It increases in strength and performance, as well as heightened awareness preparing the body to meet an emergency. Sex drive is driven by the fact that there is something that motivates our actions. Research has indicated that by putting couples in a scenario which stimulates their emotional arousal, their affiliated behaviour towards each other increases. Due to the hormonal factor, couples seem to be more affectionate towards each other when the adrenaline is produced in the body brings about arousal. Adrenaline produced in the body does not always have to be linked to a romantic type of attraction. There are times when the attraction can also be towards positive things such as a beautiful environment, bright lights, or things that catch the eye. The more aroused a person is the more attracted they are to certain sexual drives. Romantic and sexual arousal is enhanced when it also stems from a non-sexual source like exercise, a wild car drive, or a rollercoaster. Adrenaline has an effect on attraction and sexual arousal because when adrenaline increases sexual drive increases and it is a sure-fire way to pump or quicken your libido. Likewise, testosterone is one of the basic sexual stimulants that fuel sex drive in the right proportions, Testosterone is considered a male hormone, although it is produced in small amounts in women. However, it is still a significant player in the female libido. Testosterone brings sexual aggression and can boost your libido. People with a testosterone deficiency often have trouble getting aroused and have low sex interest. Testosterone makes you feel turned on and sexually alive.

Your sexual drives – believe me, there are so many things that can boost or influence your sex drive. Such as variation in men and women's sex drive. How? The stimulant in women must be steered to action before a woman will allow or will do it. Cuddles, kisses, and touching must be present to influence a woman's mood. Sexual drive in women is based on high sensitivities while most men have a strong and straightforward sexual urge. Men are more specific about what they want but to have a desirous woman in your arms you must learn the art of connecting to their emotions. Women's sexual turn-ons are more complicated than men's.

While men think and seek sex most of the time, a woman normally has to be moved in the art of feeling and connecting, romance and then they think of sex. The attitude of women to sex differs from men due to some reasons; women in nature are slower than men at doing things, so also in sex. Whereas the Bible refers to wives or women as the weaker vessel compared to men, women like to feel before acting. This nature in women must be understood to get through to their hearts. Making a woman know you care about her by making many advances toward her needs or desire is what allows them to open up to you as a person. Condemning a woman's attachment to you is shutting her and her emotion down where she cannot function toward you honestly, a woman's emotions are very important aspects of her sexual world. Desires of women are mostly triggered by emotions. Unemotional women cannot perform efficiently when it comes to sex. A woman's heart is wrapped in tenderness, the tenderer you are towards a woman the more she is attracted to you, whiles a few women nod their heads to harshness due to their personal experiences, it is not the norm in many women to love carnally. Move the heart of a woman by understanding her emotional needs and you speed her action of love towards you. This can also drive their sexual appetite towards you. Sexual drives in women are mostly in chapters where men have to read well before you can satisfy her tenderness. My sexual needs as a woman may be something I have cultivated to suit me, aside from the inborn nature of sex. I count my highlights in sex in relation to those which stir me up at different times. I need different stimulants to stir me up. Music is one of my greatest stimulants. Move me by my slow rhythm and I become more creative to move my partner to climax.

My fantasy also becomes as wild as a deer panting for water and can only be satisfied by that desirable water, if you know what I mean. There are cases where my stimulant is geared by a desirous look. Understand my stimulant and you have got me moving towards your desire. This is how it mostly works for other women as well, releasing the right moves to match up with our sexual conquests is what brings us to our knees in love and lovemaking. Social events can have an influence in one's sex life positively or negatively. The people you associate with can drive you wild. Taking this into consideration what we hear can motivate our actions, the woman's doorway to her heart is mostly through the ears, and a man who knows how to use his words right always has lots of women lining up for him because it is words that motivate women into action. There is a hidden, emotional need in a man that needs satisfaction. Men's sexual attraction to sex is steered by self-confidence in a woman and are quickly stimulated visually. The most beautiful object in a man's world is a woman. "So clean up, fix up". If you're not happy with who you are, it will show from a mile away. Men are most attracted to women who look like they're having fun with who they are, not those who are desperately seeking someone to fill a void in their lives. Be motivated to work on your aspirations. Attraction, like romantic love, works in mysterious ways. Of course, there are a number of factors that go into who we choose to be with, including personality traits, interests, values and physical appearance. Men are mostly geared by what they see, the physicality, traits like the eye, legs, body shape, facial appearance, etc.

Relationships influence us in four ways; The influence is based on physical, biological, psychological and social factors. All these come together to create our sex drive.

Your social life has control over your way of thinking because of your exposure. Less exposure leads you into shyness whiles exposure makes you competent in yourself. In every social event, there are things we can achieve to help us become more vibrant and strategized in our life. The things that surround us bring great meaning to life if we pay attention to them. Moments are missed when we lose focus of our surroundings. Whether with romantic partners, family, friends, neighbours or others, social connections can influence our biology and health.

Physical contact such as cuddles, kisses, holding of hands and caring conversations can trigger the release of hormones which can make our metabolism work quicker for sexual appetite and also for good health. This also stops the risk of developing heart disease, having a satisfying sex life may also reduce the risk of high blood pressure.

Social factors are things that affect and influence individual lifestyles such as religion, family or wealth. This makes us understand the event that opens or closes us up and also sometimes controls our habits. Social events like places we go influence us a lot. This can help us in socializing, finding and sharing. While interacting with people can boost our ego, socializing has a great prospect of converting us from our

hidden shell to the public domain. Connecting with others helps keep you in a positive mood, staying connected with others helps give you a sense of purpose and a true sense of belonging. Enjoying experiences with those who share your interests is the best call for investment.

Unaware of our hidden self-causing lack of socialisation, one may be advised to expose themself to an event that will help them getting noticed, or that will connect them to people with similar interests. Positive connection with people is important for your mental and even physical health.

There's plenty of evidence that social isolation is associated with a shorter life span, not to mention a diminishing quality of life. Understandably there are moments that cannot be traded for socialization but solitude or intimate time with each other or with one's self is very important and can improve connectivity between couples.

Only know how to live your life in balance. A healthy lifestyle is a life lived in balance, not overdoing things; apportion your time well in order to evaluate things in your life properly.

Gaining control over these areas will lead you to know, learn and celebrate your intimacy.

A right sexual drive has a massive impact on personal satisfaction.

CHAPTER THREE

The Influencer of our Sexual Drive

To thrive in anything, we must pay particular attention to such factors that can affect our growth or reduce the beauty of what we desire (quality sex). A lack of privacy or intimacy can affect our sex drive. Lack of intimacy is a great killer of sexual dreams. I stand on the notion that people who refrain from being open about intimate issues and exploration of sexual intimacy are dry of their fantasies and this reduces the chances of them falling in love with the right person and also enjoying the full benefit of romance.

Although sexual desire can change from moment to moment due to environmental factors and other issues, it's essential we master the mobility and stability of our climax. Though sexual desire is exciting and pretty important, the road to fulfilment is as equally important as the feelings. How do we get to our desired state? I seek to shed light on what influences our sexual desire.

Solomon said and I quote "He brought me to the banqueting house and his banner over me was love." This makes me understand that things don't just happen, something must happen to move other things to happen. I call this happening, THE INFLUENCER. Influence must be linked to something known or unknown and conscious efforts must be made so we know and learn more about what influences us to do what we do. These may differ from person to person due to temperament in nature and the circumstances we find ourselves.

There are four fundamental temperaments with our personality or behaviour patterns, These affect one's humour, appearance and behaviour. However, most people have mixed temperaments. Amongst these lie other traits that expose some people to be more sexually orientated.

WHAT IS TEMPERAMENT?

- Temperament is a person or animal's nature, especially as it permanently affects their behaviour.

- Temperament can also be referred to as consistent to individual differences in behaviour that are biologically based and relatively independent of learning, system of values, and attitudes.

It is the combination of mental, physical, and emotional traits of a person and their natural predisposition. It has been recorded that temperaments are found in seven forms, but we are just going to elaborate on a few. As temperaments show individual capability and natural ways of doing things, some individuals have high sexual interest whilst others are not keen on sex at all based on their temperament. The creative nature of some temperaments makes them more alert to romance than others. Nevertheless, whichever temperament you belong to that makes you rank low in sexual awareness and the enjoyment of sex can be worked on. Temperament can be a trace map that will help you to understand the sexual needs of partners. You have to know every side of your partner in order for you to enjoy each other. Let's further our study into the temperaments:

SANGUINE PERSONALITY

People (men and women) with sanguine personality type tend to be lively, talkative, easy, outgoing, optimistic, buoyant and carefree. They love adventure and have a high-risk tolerance. This personality trait is poor in tolerating boredom and will seek variety and entertainment. Judging solely by their traits may sometimes negatively affect their romantic relationship because they are prone to pleasure-seeking and constant cravings and overreacting on some issues due to their nature. On the other hand they are very creative, fantastic entertainers. Because they love pleasure, they like intense and complicated music.

PHLEGMATIC PERSONALITY

This trait is almost opposite to the sanguine. They are very introverted, very passive, which leads to a lack of ambition or sense of urgency. They are laid back, calm and unemotional, slow to warm up others (and slow to warm the bed), do not take initiative and are fiercely loyal to their friends and partners. They stick to routines. They may need quite a bit of time and patience to adapt to change, especially if it is a sudden change. Because they easily reveal their feelings, they can be hurt by rejection. This personality is also romantic.

CHOLERIC PERSONALITY

They are extroverted, quick-thinking, active, practical, strong-willed, and easily annoyed. They are self-confident, self-sufficient and very independent-minded. They are direct, to the point and firm when communicating with others. Choleric like pressure and are easily bored when things are not happening fast enough. They are bold and like to take risks. They find it easy to make decisions for themselves as well as for others and they are visionaries and seem to never run out of ideas, plans and goals. They can be very romantic and are ready for deep commitment. Instead of expressing their emotions, they will focus on pleasing their partners, getting them what they want. They like to be needed, they are very sexual, have a high sex drive but they don't sleep around, sex is very meaningful to them. They have a great sex life when they are committed to you.

MELANCHOLY PERSONALITY

They tend to become passionate and somewhat irrational when they fall in love, they are more down to earth. Sex for melancholic is a way to forget problems and relax. As a result, the intimacy with these kinds of people develops slowly; they usually have fewer sexual experiences. They nurse their connection with others and need to be a part of something bigger. Melancholic people are conventional. They have fixed moral codes and are not willing to change their values. They are also obedient to authority and believe that everybody should abide according to long-established rules and traditions. They love order, quality and quiet. They are also romantic, have a lot of incredible ideals and qualities to bring to relationships, and secretly long for ideal love.

These personalities help us to know our individual drives and strengths and also brings us to know that our moods are controlled by our natural desires or factors. In as much as I love to be driven, I want to know what or who is driving me. Our influencer can be external or internal. External factors are most of the time easy to identify compared to the internal factors which are unknown to many.

Despite the fact that you may know your temperament and may have flaws, your temperament should not stop you from enjoying what romance offers. We must do well to work on ourselves. To associate with each other we need to develop an understanding of who we really are and what brings satisfaction to our heart. There's good reason to suspect that romantic love is kept alive by something basic to our biological nature. (Our sense)

What is the meaning of sense?: A faculty by which the body perceives external stimuli; when you sense something, you know it intuitively. Sense is used in several expressions to indicate how truthful a statement is. Our sexual drive can be influenced by our senses or anxiety. Sense is the way the mind receives and processes information. How well we take in things and our understanding concerning matters. When we fall in love, chemicals associated with the reward circuit like dopamine and oxytocin flood our brain, producing a variety of physical and emotional responses, such as the racing heart, cuddles, kisses, feelings of passion, anxiety, hormone level increase during the initial phase of romance. There are other chemicals at work during romantic love which deepens the feeling of attachment and makes couples feel closer to one another before and after sex. Some chemical hormones in the brain provoke feelings of contentment, calmness and bring bonding. When you fall in love with someone, a whole host of changes are taking place in the brain and the body to create desirable effects. Falling in love causes a major hormone rush, making the heart beat faster and intense feelings of excitement.

In addition to the function of the brain, positive signals send messages from the brain to the heart, about how secure one may be in love, causing the individual to be less fearful of their partner. Love sometimes causes similar strange behaviour. Romance is the catalyst that sometimes causes the mind to be irrational. These feelings can also cause lovers to be blind to their partner's undesirable traits in the early stage of a relationship, only perceiving their partner's good qualities. Seeing an attractive face activates some part of the brain and increases blood flow to the brain for pleasure. After people have been in love for some time, the body develops a tolerance of the pleasurable chemicals. The attracted face gives the brain the way to create attachment, craving an obsession to possess love. When you are attracted to someone you can't simply stop thinking about that person. Romantic love affects the pattern of the mind. It also keeps your senses extra alert and gives us the urge to bond and attach as you love at all times even at the expense of the rest of your life. The brain has internal drug factories, which make us ecstatic and prone to happiness, when you are with the person you've falling in love with. Romantic love can strengthen your empathy. The Bible doesn't mince any words on the subject of romance (Proverbs 5:18-19 NIV) says, "may your fountain be blessed, and may you rejoice in the wife of your youth". How? (emphasis added) A loving doe, a graceful deer, may her breast satisfy you always..in essence enjoy romance. Modern experts tell us that "foreplay" also termed as "romance" before penetration is essential to a mutually satisfying experience. The scripture is strong enough as I have presented it, but it is more powerful when we understand its setting. You need ample opportunity for experimentation and enjoyment, don't rush the process of lovemaking, because unsatisfied emotions can cause furiousness when one does not reach its desirable goal.

Love makes us rise to a new level where we will normally not have reached. This becomes our motivational boost. Your motivating mechanism always lies within you, find the hidden strength within you. Motivate yourself to love, work on your stream to flow in the rivers of your sexual life. You can only make it better if you learn and work at it. Romance is beautiful in the hands of a person with understanding. I would like to discuss further the types of sex drives.

CHAPTER FOUR

The Six Senses of Romance
(Awakening Your Sensuality)

Sensuality is the ability to fully enjoy our sense of touch, smell, taste, sight and hearing. The essence of knowing about our senses, is to know how to communicate well with our senses and enjoy it. Non–verbal communication is 55% of what we say, using facial expressions, gestures, and postures.

In the field of romance we have six senses that stimulate our sex drives, which are *touch, smell, sight, hearing, taste and power of imagination.* Sensuality must not be mistaken for sexuality, they are two separate words, though sensuality can sometimes be sexual, depending on your probability to know the difference. Anything that makes you feel physically good can be sensual. Hugs, kisses, melodious sounds, a massage, having a cold bath, eating food that your soul desires can all stimulate your sensuality amongst other things. Our need to be sensual depends on the exploration of our sexual desires in many forms. We must learn to become sensual to arouse the dormant romance in us. When mindful of our sensuality it can be a tremendous sexual healing and empowerment to our lives. Consciously explore what makes you feel good and also learning the chemistry of your body, opening up yourself to new ideas and empowering your body to have a voice. Most people cannot explore their sexual power through romance because they are ashamed of their bodies. Instead of seeing your body as a sack or bag that you drag around, you must start valuing your body as a vessel of power and pleasure deeply capable of experiencing life to its maximum satisfaction. Sensuality reminds us of what it is like to completely live life and enjoy it. To be sensual is to be fully activating your human power given to you by God. Sensuality helps us to get sexuality out of our heads and into our bodies to perform. It is performance that brings fulfilment. We must learn how to use and enjoy our six senses of romance to elevate our conquest. The stimulation of the six senses in our world of romance brings a whole new knowledge of satisfaction. You have to be a more embodied human being who is capable of fully owning your sexual urges. Begin now to explore your six senses to bring out the pleasure in you.

POWER OF TOUCH (FONDLING)

One of the most important senses for human survival is touch. The feeling through touch is the most gracious of all, as it amazingly puts you in a different world of connectivity.

Touch allows us to judge how soft or firm an object is. Fingers are the most electrical way to send a message to a loved one that cannot go unrecognised. Touch cannot be taken out of romance, because it is an emblem of romance. Romance without touch cannot be called romance. According to sources "the fingers are connected to the heart," therefore, the easy way to connect to the heart is through touch. Touch can move you uncontrollably. A genuine touch from the heart is a phenomenal and extraordinary way to send a quick and genuine message to the heart or make a great impression on the mind of someone we love through touch.

Everyone desires the ability to be touched in different ways, most of all. knowing where to touch is the golden rule which cannot be ruled out from the love scene. How to touch, where to touch, and when to touch are very important in romance.

I will briefly explain how, where and when, in a few sentences on how to practise touch.

HOW?

The teasing touch does the trick for all. Approach the crotch area, keep passing around it tenderly as if you are scared to but still want to touch. Using the tactic of playing with a cat. If you reach for it, it runs away, if you tease it and stroke it – it comes to you. Move your fingertips down your partner's body from the neck to the breast to the stomach, then on the way back up, moving your fingertips. The touch must be gentle although some like it rough, in romance the slower the better. Stroke, tease touch and gently squeeze aiming for every part of the body.

WHERE?

For stimulation, each and every inch of the body is covered with nerves. These nerves are located on the body and are sensitive to touch and when stimulated they produce pleasurable sensations that can lead to increased sexual arousal. When pleasurable sensations are experienced through foreplay, the brain responds by preparing the body for sexual intercourse, increasing blood flows to particular areas and releasing a variety of hormones designed to increase the desire for sex or intimacy. Foreplay is perceived to be very important for the enjoyment of lovemaking. Sexual activity that precedes intercourse is known as foreplay. Knowing how to affectionately arouse intense excitement in your spouse for sex or lovemaking is related to romance.

Do you find yourself clueless when it comes to hitting the right buttons in romance or in bed? Here are a few places you can explore:

- The hair
- The shoulders
- The neck
- The breasts (nipples)
- The lips
- The ears
- The waist
- The palms
- The clitoris (sweet sensational)
- The penis (scrotum the honey juicy)
- Behind the knee

- Under the feet
- Down the back
- Inner thigh.

If you are passionate about providing pleasure for your partner, you're probably interested in exploring the whole body. Pleasure spots may differ from person to person. Just because some areas were not mentioned doesn't mean they wouldn't induce pleasurable sensations. It may surprise you that some areas may be the very areas that deduce the honey. You can also create a romantic scene, by setting up your environment to help you respond to it.

WHEN?

There are a lot of indicators that point out what makes a relationship strong or weak. We often overlook one of the most important and basic elements of all which is how to spend time together. Making time for each other is essential in building a successful relationship. You need to make time for each other. Time and planning must be applied to the things we do, when planning is not appropriate to the things we do, we lose value of what we have. There is a saying that time is of importance and there is time for everything. When the time is set for romance, the atmosphere must change and relate to the theme planned, setting your environment to correspond to the theme of love.

Romance has such a powerful human emotion and connection that it is currently under study because it is fundamental to most relationships. Sensational feelings of romance must be looked into, most feelings are generated from one point to another. Sensational feelings can be caused by something that happens to you especially a feeling that you cannot describe exactly but has an underlying factor.

What is a sensational feeling? Let's take it point by point and note the difference.

A sensation is a message sent from your body to your brain to let it know what's going on its how the brain is able to check on what's happening with your body. Some examples of sensations are hunger, thirst, physical pain, feeling hot, cold and joy. These all start taking place within our bodies and then move up to the brain. Whereas feelings (or emotions) are messages that start in our brains and move down to our bodies, so do romantic sensations start in the body based on reactions from touching any of the senses to release a message to the brain. The brain now processes it into feelings such as being overwhelmed, good nerves, calmness, rapid heartbeats, etc. We realise here that romance has many things to offer when it comes to touching our senses. Sensory touch is phenomenal, losing sight of one's surroundings when the right spot is hit. Master the game by touching the right place. Sensational touch brings about a reaction where it is the reason for invitation for a more savoury touch. Don't miss these sensational mixed messages of feeling to the brain sparking loving memories of romantic moments. The mind must always be involved in the spark of romance, nevertheless the thought of romance must be kept alive in the mind by the means of eventful romance being replayed in the mind from time to time. This brings me to the subject of the power of imagination.

POWER OF IMAGINATION

Some may think romantic attraction just happens, oh no it does not just happen. You must desire it and work on it. Being sexy and being romantic takes a little hard work and forward planning by taking your power of imagination serious. Use the power of imagination to visualize vividly what you would like to be successful in. Allow your imagination to complement your action and hard work. When you visualize, there should be no doubt at all in the outcome towards success and excellence. Imagination and creativity are an important part of human life. The incredible power of your own imagination is your greatest asset. Imagination is more important than knowledge. Every idea and all innovative solutions first originated in someone's mind as a question or imagination. Casting our minds back as children, there were things we created with great excitement, we also had wild imaginations of doing things, some were without base, funny, and also didn't make sense. Just cast your mind back and remember one of your childhood memories, grab one funny moment that strikes your mind. What was it? Do you have fresh memories about it? How does it make you feel? Of course, moments like that are precious and priceless. It was our sense of achievement for being creative enough to invent something, but as we grew older, we lost this creative ability and became more rigid without a drive of productivity. The right sense of creativity helps us to express ourselves such as feelings and thoughts. Few of as think of creativity as a primary and critical relationship skill. Explore creative options that might enrich your love life or your marriage. If the picture of your relationship doesn't look the way you want it to be , make some changes, add the attitude of responsibility, compassion and love, that will bring you to the glaze of beauty. Know that creativity is more than arts and crafts, decorating, music, designing, drawing, and writing. It's also about imagination, thinking outside the box and reinventing something great for your relationship. Imagination helps us integrate our experience and our minds into learning. Research shows that just imagining something can have the same effect as actually doing it. Self-imagination can lead your mind to places where you will be filled with memories of sweet butterflies, a waterfall, etc. The power of imagination turns the light on in our minds, brings glimmer in the heart. With imagination, you could see the essence of creation. Without imagination, it would be very difficult to be creative in our relationships. Creativity in relationships is very vital for the longevity of the relationship. Being with someone for a long time can sometimes become boring if we do not look at refreshing the relationship. Everyone has creative imagination and there is the need to improve upon your creative abilities by learning how to use our inner power for our advancement and happiness. Creativity relies on imagination to broaden your horizon. These are the best ways to programme yourself for a shift. As good imagination leads to fulfilment in a relationship so does wrong imagination lead to a sour taste in your mouth. Look! There is much more going on in the brain than you can imagine.

Five years of marriage broke because a of wrong feeding of the mind on something unhealthy. Let us find out happened.

On one fateful afternoon or do I say one unfortunate day, a man returned from work earlier than usual expecting to meet his wife at home for a quickie (you know what I mean?) a quick sex. With disappointment he found out she was not at home. Martin decided to call his friend Andrew to talk with him,

Martin: How are you Andrew?

Andrew: Charlie boys are down this week and the weather is too hot today, hmmmmmmm.

Martin: The weather is hotter at my end than yours, I need a way out.

Andrew: Martin I sense something is eating you up.

Martin: Waters are boiling, I need something to cool me down

Andrew: Spill the beans bro! Is wifey ok? What about the children?

Martin: Yeah, they are all fine. But I am not fine at all, do you know Mercy passed by the office today?

Andrew: Mercy again! What happened?

Martin: We engaged in a few minutes conversation just like old times, then everything turned, I started feeling horny, the moment I looked into her eyes, you know her presence always stirs me up, I tried to compose myself but I couldn't, we kissed. That's how far I went but you know I have always wanted more, bro I can't get that moment out of my mind.

Andrew: In your office! Bro! Fire is stirring up and we need to quench it. This must stop! How do we deal with it? It's been about 3 to 4 years now and you can't get her out of your mind?

Martin: Charlie, things are worse now.

Andrew: How? What do you mean Martin?

Martin: Did you know that close to a year and half now I have always had to imagine Mercy before I could make love to my wife?

Andrew: You don't mean it.

Martin: Oh yes, I do! You know her soft voice, her skin, her touch is phenomenal. I imagine her every time in my mind, I can't get her out of my mind. I still fancy her. The worst part of it all this is, she is the one I imagine before I can make love to my wife every day. She is stuck in my brain.

Andrew: Boy you need to see a psychologist.

Martin: Deliverance is what I need most Andrew.

At the end of that statement Martin felt a big cushion land on his head and a loud angry voice from behind him saying, "You need a divorce!" and that is exactly what am going to give you. Martin turned around and there was his wife. Martin, trembling asked the wife, "Honey how long have you been listening?" When she didn't reply he continued, "Honey I can explain,!... I...., I...". You can imagine how this ended. Divorce was the final stage. The power of imagination is very powerful. The wrong use of it can open up doors to great problems. Your thoughts must be controlled in the field of romance and also used to enhance the beauty of love. Using your mind or imagination to create what you desire is more suitable for a healthy relationship. Have you come across a man or woman who has been well satisfied by their lover? They begin to imagine or replay the event in their mind, giggling, smiling and glowing, enjoying the moment over and over again and also making plans for a further game or rematch if I may say. You can use imagination in the field of romance to create a seductive moment, where you plan to improve on your previous involvement by luring your partner into another more intense or daring adventure. The unseen world of imagination brings you into a place of creativity. Seduction makes romance authentic.

What is seduction? In case you may think it is a wrong word to use, seduction comes from the Latin word "seducer" or to "lead away". This means leading, tempting, attracting, or luring someone to the very place of compromise with enticing words or creating an erotic environment. Seductiveness can be complicated if not handled well. On the other hand, it is a great tool in matchmaking. Without seductiveness, there is no captivation and intrigue. Seduction is a powerful tool or weapon you can use in the grounds of romance which will bring joy to your heart when you understanding what to do. Seduction is a tool that emanates from our imagination, projecting one's thoughts into action. The seductive element in another person is not always a leading way to going astray, but rather the opposite: it is someone who leads us to understand ourselves better, someone who seems to understand us and recognize our uniqueness and what we have to offer. Seduction often lies in someone's understanding of our dreams and our innermost desires.

THE POWER OF HEARING

The ability to hear enables us to connect to the world for many very important reasons. Hearing helps us to communicate in a way that none of our other senses can achieve. Of all the five senses, our hearing is perhaps the most precious of them all, if we lose it, we lose contact with people we love. To communicate with other people is heavily dependent on our ability to understand what is being said, misunderstanding what has been said can be very frustrating for both the listener and speaker and can make socialising with family very difficult. Too often misconceptions relating to a relationship can be greatly reduced if we try to listen more and understand before we take action. As important as communicating with other people certainly is, listen to the one you are communicating with matters for all the pleasure it can bring and the difference it can make to our quality of life and love. Listening to music, television and radio, going to the cinema or theatre, attending a place of worship, going to meetings to learn or simply for pleasure as well as listening to the sound of nature can be affected by the state of hearing.

Whilst we are all individuals and have different interests and needs, hearing well is part of enjoying life to the fullest. Relationships can be managed wrongly by our unpreparedness to tune our hearts to hear our needs and that of our partner. Hearing the right sound, pitch, or tone of voice can boost our sexual desire for one another in the love scene whilst giving in to inappropriate hearing can also destroy the melody in a relationship. Can you work on your hearing to make relationships better? Yes, you can but only if you begin to pay attention and listen to the needs or wants of who you relate to.

Love has a voice and it can be heard, it is the tone our heart hears, the voice that brings calmness to our soul.

Perhaps you and your partner will enjoy exchanging erotic utterances whispered into each other's ears or expressed out loud to express enjoyment.

THE POWER OF SPEECH (SEDUCTIVE VOICE OR TONE)

One captivating way to sustain love or romance is through your voice. The tone of your voice plays a major role in connectivity to the innermost heart of a person. A warm voice has its distinctive part to play, whereas the cold voice or tone will show restrain from good manners. Hearing an appealing voice can heighten our feelings of attraction. Vocal attractiveness and inter-activeness may serve as an important cue to physical attractiveness. Both men and women with attractive voices tend to have people flopping around them whereas sexual advancement commences earlier in their lives and they tend to have more sex partners because how well they use their word to lure or listen to their heart. These sexual advantages may be due to their vocal attractiveness or to their associated physical attractiveness of how they use their voice to convince and soothing the heart suitors. Though sexy voices may heighten our initial attraction to a partner, the strategy you may want to use might depend on who you are dealing with, some like calm voices and others like high pitch. The effects of vocal attractiveness will be more or less pronounced than if you meet in person and experience it. In most cases people with a calm voice seem to be noticed for their humility whilst those with high pitched voices are associated with something else such as being rude or not well-mannered. A balanced way of using your voice is a core mark of our daily activities. Using the seductive voice in the wrong scene may also cost you or create wrong the impression about you being slothful. The boosting factor of romance is how you use your voice. People are found to change their voices when speaking to someone they find attractive. Men's voices vary more in pitch and go lower when they are speaking to a woman they are attracted to. Your tone of voice can take another turn in romance when you induce sweetness in your voice. Collectively people may use your voice to associate with your character.

There are different types of voices or tones for different occasions. Many people are familiar with the statement "it's not what you say but how you say it." How you say something really matters especially in the area of intimate relationships. The tone of voice we use can positively or negatively affect our interaction with others, particularly with those close to us. How you speak and what you and your partner say to each other, greatly impacts your emotion and the quality of your relationships. What makes communication different lies in the tone of voice we choose when we communicate with others. Pay attention to how particular voice tones affect your mood and emotions. Most of us don't pay enough attention to how our tone of voice affects our interaction with others in different ways. It may bring excitement and sadness to the people around us. We can do better with our voice when we take particular notice of the different tones and the appropriate way to use it.

There are different ways to get your message across without saying a word, as there many ways to kill a cat as the idiom goes. If you want something you must find a way to get it. Now, here are a few ways to pass your message across without the medium of a word. There are different types of tones to use in a romantic setting. Let me share three tones you can use to your advantage:

BREATHING TONES

THE BREATHING TONE: Breathing can be used as a nonverbal approach to communicate. I have listed and explained the three forms:

THE SEMI-BREATHING TONE: sends a message or signal of longing to your partner. Breathing and holding yourself half-way to stop full breathing will send a message like, *I miss you, I need you now, am calling for intimacy, I am sexually aroused now. Don't keep me waiting.* These are words that can be spoken without words and it is better said when you apply your breathing tone to pass this message across. It is more fulfilling and intriguing and most importantly very romantic.

THE SHORT SHAPE BREATHING: also communicating the word, of dissatisfaction, worry, pain, or hurt. In this way, you are able to tell of your disagreement without any abusive words. This manner of communication controls the temper of the offended from using wrong words. Offence happens in any relationship but it the choice of words that wound or heal the heart.

FULL BREATHING TONES: full breathing tone is in its maximum capacity to tell of how exhausted one is. Tiredness can slow down any performance, no matter how good someone is when they are tired. This form of communication is the simplest form to pass on your message. Communication with signs is the most efficient way to sweeten your love vocabulary. Communication in the romantic sense is what calls for action, and this can be done well with non-verbal words. This is because, non-verbal words set the emotion rolling and gets the heart looking for what the other heart is saying. Saying things with words has its place in love but the best of all is using signs and tokens to communicate your needs. Communication must be done one way or the other in relationships. Using different means to communicate spices your love and refreshes the moment of communication with something to look forward to, and it takes the boredom away. Knowing your partner's signal talk is a plus. Practise and use your breathing tone to communicate, as it is the most efficient way to communicate without error if you are well understood.

THE POWER OF SIGHT (THE GAZE FACTOR)

There is a saying that goes seeing is believing. There is also a reason we talk about love at first sight. Love at first sight is not easy to explain, actually how can we fall in love after one quick glance? Let me make sense of this trusted statement. What you see is what attracts you. Sight aids affection because the eyes control your mind.

A first impression is what leads us to make further advancement. When the mind receives information from the eye of a very erotic sight of something desirable the mind adjusts itself to probe intently. Sight is the divine radar to transmitting love.

Sight aids feelings thereby you are able to pursue what you have seen, to touch and to behold. It is also said that what is seen and held, you don't forget.

Sight is your observance and the acknowledgement of negative and positive changes in a person. Eye contact is vital to our encounters with others. The eyes are the windows to one's soul. Gazing into the eyes of the one you love is the most magical and intimate moment of all. Serotonin is released when we meet someone. When we find them attractive and in turn has a huge impact on our feelings throughout the initial stages of a relationship.

The long gazes can make people feel more attracted to each other. Eye contact also increases affection and sexual connection or arousal. Using eye contact in arousing the set-up mood for lovemaking should not be taken for granted. Women and men are equally stimulated by erotic images. In order for men to be turned on or relate to the opposite sex, they must know what attracts them because they are visual creatures and are turned on by what they see. Sight is the sense that the brain relies on for essential information. Without the ability to see, the brain cannot easily navigate its environment, we receive information for the brain to process the information we have received.

THE POWER OF SCENT (THE SMELL)

Smell is most often an overlooked sense. Smell is one of our most primitive senses. It is said to be the sense that can evokes memories.

Smell and taste work more closely together than any of the other senses, as we are more likely to enjoy foods that we perceive to have a pleasant aroma. Psychologists have also suggested that a particular smell associated with time and/or place can stimulate a person's ability to recall a memory. There are two main scents. Appropriate or inappropriate, pleasant or unpleasant scent that can make a great difference in our love life or romance. Another function of smell comes into play when people assess the attractiveness of a potential partner. This can influence a person's perception of another physical appearance. Unpleasant smells help humans avoid consuming inedible or rotten foods.

Pay proper attention to scent as it can be a turn-on or turn-off in the setting of romance.

APPROPRIATE SCENT (THE SCENT OF DESIRE)

Physical attraction has a major strength in our smell though we may remain partially oblivious to scent signals we send and receive. Scent helps us connect to the one the soul desires.

The nose plays a much larger role in our social lives than we realise. Smell is one of the most important senses. It helps us to make sense of our environment, scent links us to memories, emotions and interactions with other people – encouraging us to draw closer or pull back. The nose also deserves much more credit for our pleasure, especially when it comes to our taste. Most of the time, it is our smell that draws us closer to what we want to taste or eat. In the same way, smell will draw you closer to the one you would like to be with or stay with. Natural body odours play a major role in relationships as most people choose their partners by being attracted to their scent. As a result, smell can trigger thoughts and behaviours. Smell communicates something deeper than what we just see, it brings connectivity and also connects the soul to longing desires. Appropriate smell is very powerful.

In relation to the above, a romantic scent generates a great part of attraction in relationships. An appropriate scent signals a great bond between men and women and also increases chemistry. When you're turned on by your partner's scent, taking a deep sniff of his or her chest, back of the neck, etc., it takes you to a whole realm of sensitivity and the erotic moment you can't just let go. Deliberate smelling of a romantic partner's clothes whiles they are away, brings the feeling of comfort and draws you closer to cherished memories of your partner by the sensation.

Smells can trigger your memory and fragrance is the means by which we can make a first impression, and also leave a lasting one. Scents are traditionally associated with romance. So, if you wear a certain fragrance regularly, someone you are dating, or a spouse might feel comfortable or happy when smelling it because it can remind them of you or vice versa.

A fragrance is meant to be a hint of who you are and to make a subtle impression. You want to be noticed when you walk into a room and your personality be reflected in your sweet aroma. Use good or mild scented perfume to create effect.

A fragrance can be your signature that will give you a bit of sensuality which adds to the mystery of sexual attraction.

Where is the best place to wear perfume for maximum effect?

I think our wrists and necks which are pulse points, allow the oils of the perfume to really warm up and diffuse more around us when we wear perfume.

Applying your fragrance on pulse points where heat concentrates, such as your wrist, collar bones, and neckline will also ensure your fragrance blends well with your natural aroma. Make sure not to overdo it though as too much perfume can be distracting to your partner.

Using aphrodisiac aromas in the bedroom can be a fun and sensual part of aiding one's foreplay. Aphrodisiac scents are fragrances that arouse sexual instinct by increasing desire, pleasure or performance. They symbolize true love in affairs of the heart, cementing fragrance as a very romantic emotional love potion to romance.

INAPPROPRIATE SMELL (BEWARE OF OFFENSIVE ODOURS)

A wife began to worry when her sexual life kept sinking. She then decided to call a meeting between her and the husband. On several attempts, she failed to resolve the issue because anytime the matter arose the husband would give an excuse to leave the discussion. He made himself unavailable to talk with, he was the first to wake up and leave the house whiles his wife was still sleeping. He got back home late to eat his dinner, have his shower and went straight to bed. This routine continued for four to five months without them having time for each other. The woman became so moody and this affected her mind and her way of doing things by slowing her down. She became a habitual latecomer to work and to every occasion. Depression set in and mistakes were the order of her day. One day she came back from work far more depressed, oppressed and dejected. Oh! what an awful time in her life; she then lost her job. She couldn't believe it, what a nightmare. That job became her newly found companion since the way to the husband's heart seemed to be blocked to all her advances. She felt betrayed by losing everything she loved, and this caused more pain when she thought about it, her mind was tortured. Nothing was working for her and all she wanted to do was stay in bed and cry her eyes out.

She couldn't communicate with her husband since he was never at home and had taken to unusual long days travelling. This lady endured the pain and suffered the humiliation all by herself. She one day gathered the courage to ask for a divorce from her husband as soon as he returned from his travelling. Yeah, this decision was geared by a movie she watched where a lady who was maltreated by the husband got divorced. She thought to herself, this is the way out. I have got the solution now.

Before the return of her husband, Mrs Oduro made a call to their counsellor to announce her decision to divorce. The counsellor probed to know the reason why she had chosen to divorce. She then narrated everything systematically to

Mrs Ford, the counsellor. Upon hearing this Mrs Ford felt so sorry for her and all that she had gone through. She tried her best to console and assured her that she was available anytime she felt like talking.

She also promised to have a word with the husband and resolve matters. Two weeks after the discussion with Mrs Ford, Mr Oduro arrived from his trip.

Mrs Oduro quickly sneaked out like a mouse with delicious cheese, to make a phone call to Mrs Ford to alert her of the arrival of Mr Oduro. Mrs Ford then made a phone call to Mr Oduro and arranged for a suitable date to meet for a discussion. The date was set. Mrs Oduro was a bit relieved and said finally I'm going to divorce this man and have my peace. As all was set and done the appointed day came. They met in the office of Mrs Ford as they travelled individually. Mr Oduro was the first to arrive 5 minutes later Mrs Oduro also arrived. The receptionist gave them individual seats. The counsellor called Mr Oduro to her inner office without delay. Mrs Ford asked what was going on in their marriage.

Mr Ford finally spoke out and revealed, "I have of late not been around and have not being involved in my marital duties due to the fact that something is bothering me." Mrs Ford asked what the matter was. He replied, "My wife has developed excessive and offensive body odour where I find it hard to manage. I once spoke to her about it but she did nothing and told me, my words were offensive to her and it simply drew us apart. I find it difficult to sleep with her in the same bed and make love to her. This is my reason for withdrawal, a strong offensive odour." Mrs Ford thanked

Mr Oduro for opening up and sharing. She addressed that being silent is not the best choice but find a convenient way to talk to her. In addition, the choice of words you use in addressing an issue is very important. "Mr Oduro, you could have bought a perfume or deodorant specially for her to use which is another way to help your wife deal with the bad odour." Mr Oduro not knowing what to do apologised to Mrs Ford. She then called Mrs Oduro in for a discussion. Mr Oduro rendered a sincere apology to his dear wife for not being there and also for not attending to his marital duties. A few minutes after Mrs Oduro entered the room, Mrs Ford had to open all the windows for fresh air. I believe you know what was going on? Because Mrs Oduro has a very bad body odour. Mr Oduro was right, the smell was really bad. Mrs Ford asked Mr Oduro to wait outside. Mrs Ford now began to talk with Mrs Oduro about all that her husband has said about the smell and what she has also experienced in the few minutes when she entered. Mrs Oduro bowed her head in regret and shame saying, "I am sorry ...I didn't know I...I...I"

She said, "I am ready to work on myself." A few tutorials were given to her by Mrs Ford, to deal with the problem. Like washing well and applying an underarm antiperspirant or deodorant, changing and washing your clothes regularly, shaving all private areas where necessary, thoroughly. Brushing her teeth regularly (twice a day) such as morning and evening or after having a meal. Watch her diet (You are what you eat, some foods can contribute to causing body odour) and wear cotton fabric (The kind of fabric you wear can also affect how much you sweat.) these tips can also help in dealing with body odour to anyone who relates to such issues. Unfortunately, some people experience more difficulty in this area than others, but there is no excuse for bad breath, body odour, or any other offensive smells today. A thoughtful lover will prepare for lovemaking by taking frequent baths, using effective deodorant, and practising good oral hygiene.

Imagine being welcomed with a very strong bad body odour from your partner. This makes you feel uncomfortable and affect your advances to any attachment and attraction.

Scent can be a deal-breaker so regardless of how uncomfortable it may be, deal with it when prompted.

Chapter Five

Setting Up your Environment for Romance

Everyone has sexual fantasies but rarely do couples get to the place where they feel comfortable sharing those desires. If you want to keep the spark and passion in your relationship alive, making the effort to set the mood is the key to lasting fulfilment in any mutual relationship. Setting the mood has been the number one thing people neglect to do to keep their relationship sweet and spicy. Creating or planning a romantic environment is what we forget to do but love to enjoy. Most couples live daydreaming about the improvement of their love affair yet fail to plan for it. You must know that work comes before enjoyment. Anything you want to enjoy you must put it to work.

A suitable romantic environment can play an essential role in your sex life as it awakens and makes your senses more responsive. Creating magical moments in our relationship is something everyone thinks or dreams about, but few people dare to create it. Perhaps it's because they actually can't think of exactly what to do. To have a sizzling sex life there is a road map called Romance that needs to be followed. Romance doesn't always start in the bedroom but in an environment that calls for it. If romance will grow it must be given time and space which will create a conducive and responsive atmosphere. To spice up love, we must put into consideration the factors or the things that come together to bring the emblem of love which is affectionate, emotion and caring, etc., there is a saying that you can't create a connection with a person, connection with someone is either there or it isn't, although this statement may be true to an extent, I believe you can create the environment where you can induce connections or reveal and revive the hidden feelings lying dormant in us. Being in the right mood and creating the right environment can affect other aspects of our mood positively. Also creating the right environment can increase good feelings and make couples let down their guard and connect on a deeper level. Creating a romantic atmosphere sometimes depends on the occasion or the weather. In some cases, the weather is a light-up force that sparks the mood of romance, hence planning must be made towards it. Whilst an atmosphere of romance should be planned, there are other moods that call for immediate action, hence time to plan will disrupt things. Move by the desire and embrace the moment of demand. Also note, preparation of a romantic event is something personal and that couples may have their own ideas, tastes and styles.

You have to create an atmosphere that is relaxing and comfortable yet filled with the right dose of love and affection at the same time. I say the right dose because you don't want to overdo things to dim affairs. Consideration must be put into our plan of action as to how, when, where and who you are creating that atmosphere for. Now the purpose of creating the love scene is to increase romance and to allow proper connection. Making it our most beneficial factor as to spend time with the one you love, with a welcoming mood and the intention of enjoying each other. Remember romance can happen everywhere not just in your bedroom, so don't plan just for the bedroom but all your surroundings. With this in mind, you are ready to set up your plans. A trip away with just the two of you allows you to spend time together without the interruption of work, timetables, children and household chores.

PLANNING

A surprise romantic getaway is the perfect way to show your partner how much they mean to you. For any plan to work, you must take into consideration these things: when planning an intimate dinner or other events you must use your creative imagination and ingenuity to arouse the senses with beautiful sights, sounds, flavours, aromas, etc. Prior to the plan you must consider these four guidelines to enable you to plan well.

1. **Who** – (The person or your guest) When it comes to relationships we all have our vision of what we expect, how you want someone, who makes us laugh, feel good, the side that really matters is how well does your partner meets your emotional needs. In relationships, everyone has the same basic emotional needs to ensure not only the survival of the relationship but their survival as an individual. Your partner should be providing support in the areas important to your spouse. When your needs remain unaddressed or unmet, it results naturally in hurt, resentment, irritation, annoyance, anger, etc. Plan to suit the emotional needs of your partner. There are people who do a lot trying to fulfil the needs of their companion but fail to do the most important things or never meet that need. Why? Because their focus is on the wrong things, such as pleasing themselves or placing themselves above their partners. You don't get to know your partner's needs if you don't communicate or pay attention.

Communicate so that you can understand your partner's needs. Or do I say learn to master your partner's needs and respond in the appropriate time and manner. Sometimes your needs will conflict with one another and you must talk about it, negotiate or come to a compromise together.

However, other needs of your partner are based on regularly connecting, where keeping in touch is necessary. If our partners are unwilling to meet our needs the relationship suffers, in other words, if we are also unwilling to meet our partner's needs the outcome remains the same. Working to meet each other's needs is what cements the relationship.

Every thriving relationship must ask and know these basic questions about their partner's needs:

- What does he/she need in a relationship in order to feel loved, secure, happy, or fulfilled?
- What is his/her purpose in life driven by?
- What are their core values?
- How well does he/she pay attention to detail?
- Am I ready to meet these needs?

Know this, and by applying the above questions and answers they could help every matured relationship to prolong in excitement or do I say live on cloud 9.

To every occasion planning, apply the answers above and you will engage in something exciting with your spouse. Planning cannot be effective unless it is done with consideration and done together.

2. **WHEN** – (Time or timing): Consideration of time spent must be put into your action plan. For instance, you don't want to plan for a romantic getaway for weeks and realise you or your partner don't have the luxury of that time. For instance, you can plan for a one-hour romantic moment, which is within your reach and it can leave a lifetime memory in your heart. In as much as time is of the essence, you must make time for romance in your relationship because romance will not just happen. Consider the duration of your time to plan and use it wisely. Every minute is important as wrong timing can destroy the romance. Consider wrong timing to being just doing things to suit you without thinking of the other party. Consideration must be made for both. Also, wrong

timing is when there is no consideration for the mood or feelings concerning your partner, the right state of mind and attitude to achieve romance. Make sure planning is processed when your partner is in the right frame of mind. The right timing can also be freeing your lover from stress or grief or just a time to "loveciate". Whichever your choice of time is, make sure it is appropriate to share love.

3. **How** – (what to do and how to go about it) there are many ways to plan for a getaway, where you can create a special moment out of little details or a pleasant surprise. A surprise can be as large as an unanticipated trip or as small as a secret gift. If you are feeling clueless, call a trusted friend or a family member and ask for advice. The more information you have, the better decision you can make.

Whiles you're figuring out how much of a surprise you want your trip to be, here is some information to consider. To plan for a surprise, note! You much know how well your partner can handle a surprise. If your partner likes spontaneity and surprises, an unexpected trip could be the best present. Planning for something new for both of you can be really fun. Sometimes a weekend away from your normal routine is all it takes to jump-start the romance in a relationship.

Surprises must be kept secret, the best of romantic surprises have been ruined by a slip of tongue either by you or a friend. Can you keep a secret? If you can, plan for a surprise package, if not, choose an open trip where your partner is aware, inform your lover three to four weeks in advance, discuss the trip together and ultimately create your own romance. Planning can bring hitches here and there, so you must be in the best frame of the romantic mind. It helps you to laugh at lapses along the way.

PLANNING FOR GETAWAY NEEDS

(Your responsibility for the surprise trip)

Book time off work – (arrange for your partner to have time off, appropriate time off work will help couples to plan well for their trip.)

- **Travelling arrangements** – collecting passports, tickets, boarding passes amongst others.

- **Childcare** (optional – if the couple has children getting someone to care for the children while you are away should be considered.)

- **Accommodation** – (a suitable living accommodation or stay in a hotel, the park, weekend house to book, etc.)

- **Activities** – (Spa, mountain climbing, a walk in the night or early morning, cinema, swimming, etc. Keep in mind the purpose of the trip and leave time for relaxation and connection) plan one or two activities for each day.

- **Mobility** – (Car rental, personal car, train, boat, bus, airplane)Your mobility in and out of the venue must be taken into account if you are to visit different places. Rent a car to drive by yourself or book a cab each time you want to leave the venue for sightseeing.

- **Packing your bags** – packing of clothes. You must pack well. Inadequate packing can ruin your enjoyment when you get to your destination and find the things you need aren't available. It is better to pack more things you need than what you don't need or less of what you need. Useful essentials depend on what kind of trip you're about to embark on. If your trip is a surprise, pack without your partner's knowledge.

  - Passport
  - Phone charger
  - Shoes/flip flops
  - Socks
  - Underwear (pack enough)
  - Sun cream
  - Sleeping bag
  - Water bottle
  - Snacks (pack a few of your favourite biscuits or chocolate)
  - Camera and charger
  - Torchlight
  - Toiletries (deodorant, shampoo, conditioner, body wash, towel, moisturizer, toothbrush, toothpaste, razor and nail clipper, emergency sanitary pads)
  - Medicine/first aid kit
  - Clothes (Taking into consideration the weather since that can be unpredictable)
  - Bedding

THINGS TO GET

- Candles or torches to set the mood.
- Sweets or candies (chocolate)
- Massage oil
- Bubble bath soap
- Favourite food or fruit
- CD player or playlist with soft music, sexy tunes that you both love
- Your outfit – something that makes you feel confident and sexy. Don't force yourself to wear things that are too tight to take off. Try new things like edible panties
- Fun Games – (naughty cards or Pick and act) feel free to invent your own games (play by your own rules) don't be too competitive
- A picnic blanket and Mat
- Utensils

4. **WHERE** – (Place or environment): Another thing to consider in your plan is the place. Plan your romantic getaway to fit a particular place. The place can also be known as the venue of romance. Your trip should be special to both of you. One way to find sure-fire in romance is to choose a destination that's special and interesting to you as a couple. Choose a city, a town, a location that played a key role in the evolution of your relationship or even a place you've talked about for years but have never been. The fact is whether you choose a familiar place or someplace new, the key is to create an experience that will be enjoyed by both

of you. Caution! Do not book or choose a place of risk or a hotel whose services can interrupt your enjoyment such as bad food or poor services that can ruin a special dinner and moment. A romantic venue should be a place where you can give your partner 100% attention. Therefore, have your phone but don't be interrupted by it.

INDOORS

Set the mood by playing some soft, romantic music, classical music is usually a safe bet, so is jazz and soul.

- Fill the room with a dramatic array of flowers to add visual interest as well as inexpensive elegance.

- Please note there are people who are allergic to particular flowers and that must be taken into account which flowers to pick for the occasion.

- There must be enough ventilation to avoid excessive sweating and dampness.

Possibly prolonged exposure to high levels of indoor dampness in some locations is not good for the lungs which can expose one to infections, potentially increasing the risk of depression.

- Light the room up with either bright, slow-burning candles or, if possible, the glow from a fireplace to add a warm, intimate tone to the moment.

- Prepare a tasty meal to the taste of your partner taking allergies into consideration. In addition, the presentation of food must be well decorated.

- Choice of wine or any drink to taste, consider the weather and make plans for which drink, beverage, or fruits are suitable to serve and how to serve them.

- Indoor sounds must be controlled.

- Music or sound should not fluctuate but take a particular pattern in other to smoothen the heart.

Regulations of songs must be based on choice of songs to allow music to flow. Don't turn on the radio. As some songs may not be appropriate for your night or day, radio commercials can really kill the mood.

- Reflected colours or bright colours in mind for your setting will help promote sound mind. Colours such as red, yellow and orange are warm and spicy, and can serve as a backdrop to romance in the bedroom.

- Erotic images on the wall will help in setting the romantic mood or arousing the mood.

- Creative ideas like changing parts of your home for different purposes such as decorating your balcony or living room as a bedroom, or kitchen or dining area as a professional or proper restaurant.

- Also making other areas conducive to enjoying a quickie (sex) such as bathroom, stairs, kitchen, living room, etc., with style. Share a hot bath. Watch a movie together.

OUTDOOR: (QUIET AND ENCLOSED SPACE)

Take advantage of the moment outside the bedroom to heat up things. The success of any outdoor event is at the mercy of the weather. Plan your outdoor event being mindful of the weather, sunset, full moon, rain, etc. The weather can spark your moment of romance outside. Bear in mind the place of the event. It must be suitable for preparation, for example, your backyard, garden, park, beach, around waterfalls, in the woods, in the car, sensual sights and any place of your choice that can be a spotlight for romance, trying something new each time. Mandatorily, when planning an outdoor event or romance outside your environment or home you must know the rule of your choice location before setting it as a place for romance or obtain the necessary permit. When you fail to prepare for any eventuality, it could spell disaster for your event. Put your backup plan together if the unexpected happens. Uncontrolled noise may ruin your moment of romance and these must be checked, as the purpose of the event is to relax and spend time with each other and to connect.

SUMMARY AND HIGHLIGHTS

THE SECRETS OF ROMANCE – I hope the love, wisdom, and insights that come from this book will make you fall in love with it. The book helps reflect the ideas, formation and restoration of romance characterised by the genuineness of oneself. The information and the reflection of THE SECRETS OF ROMANCE is embodied in our day-to-day activities which can help us become better and enjoy the best of our relationships. Lessons learnt here can be life-changing. There are guidelines, instructions, objectives, leaving you with ideas for your reference.

THE SECRETS OF ROMANCE is just for you and everyone who delights in making their romantic side more special, visible and dazzling. Your mind-set in reading THE SECRETS OF ROMANCE is more important here. Don't just blaze through the pages as fast as you can but rather read to reflect, as if you are going to teach on the subject. This is how you can better retain the information in this book. When you finish reading this book I hope you would agree with me that romance is a very important part of every relationship that must be kept alive.

Romance can be kept alive if you know what to do, manipulating our way through things does not help any more than just bring misunderstanding and dissatisfaction. This is why you don't have to suffer anymore. A good read through THE SECRETS OF ROMANCE can equip you with the tools to minimize your fears of letting ourselves go, learning to live with our desires coming to pass by doing what is necessary. Understanding your needs as a person and the needs of your beloved will always present itself in your courtship, relationship, or marriage.

The nitty-gritty demands of how we should live to enhance our love affairs with balance in knowing what to do and doing it, will help us to attain the desired results in our romantic lives. The phrase "A bird in the hand is worth two in the bush" is to say, cherish what is in your hands by working on it (such as a love affair, your lover, or your romantic life) than living unrealistically. We look and admire thriving relationships but fail to work on ours to become the driving force of others' admiration. Your love or romantic side can be beautified if you take time to work on it. Smiling through life is what you do with what you have.

THE SECRETS OF ROMANCE has highlighted many points and views for your enhancement, just to mention a few. This highlight has drawn our attention to understudy relevant information to help your memory to store important information. Giving ear to these highlights could help you to apply what is being said with considerable thought.

MY HIGHLIGHTS

YOUR SEXUAL DRIVE – a lack of privacy or intimacy can affect our sex drive, and can be a great killer of sexual dreams. Although sexual desire can change from moment to moment due to environmental factors and other issues, it's essential we master the mobility and stability of our climax.

YOUR REALM OF FANTASY – Love is the guiding force that makes it possible for you to traverse your realm of fantasy. Your realm of fantasy should therefore make it easier to spice up your love life.

YOUR RHYTHM – Your rhythm is your map to trace your heart. Rhythm in romance is a great combination to steal the heart.

YOUR LOVE LANGUAGE – Simply refers to the way we express ourselves when we want to demonstrate affection or sex romantically.

TEMPERAMENTS – As temperaments show individual capability and natural ways of doing things, some individuals have high sexual interest whilst others are not keen on sex at all due to their temperament. The creative nature of some temperaments makes them more alert to romance than others. Nevertheless, whichever temperament you belong to that makes you rank low in sexual awareness and the enjoyment of sex can be worked on. Temperament can be a trace map that can help you to understand the sexual needs of partners. You have to know every side of your partner in order for you to enjoy each other.

YOUR SENSES – Awakening your sensuality through your senses to enjoy the best of what sexuality will offer. The strength of your relationship depends on the consistency of sexual involvement together, discovering, understanding and enjoying your romantic lifestyle. Make note of how each of your senses is stimulated to function and the importance of your senses in your romantic life. Your six senses respond quickly to love when they have been activated. The success of your dream, romantic life is highlighted by how approachable your senses are, training your senses to respond to your needs of love is your responsibility.

ENJOY THE BEST OF YOUR ROMANTIC LIFE.
The end

Notes